Also by John McCain
available from Random House Large Print

WORTH THE FIGHTING FOR

FAITH OF MY FATHERS

RANDOM HOUSE
HOUSE
LARGE
PRINT

Why Courage Matters

Why Courage Matters

THE WAY TO
A BRAVER LIFE

JOHN McCAIN
with Mark Salter

The Library of Congress has established
a Cataloging-in-Publication record
for this title.

0-375-43234-5

www.randomlargeprint.com

FIRST LARGE PRINT EDITION

10   9   8   7   6   5   4   3   2   1

This Large Print edition published in
accord with the standards of the N.A.V.H.

In memory of the valor of

John S. McCain Jr.

and Chester D. Salter Jr.

To have courage for whatever comes in life—
everything lies in that.

— MOTHER TERESA

Why Courage Matters

*Master Sergeant Roy P. Benavidez
during funeral ceremonies at
Arlington National Cemetery,
1984.*

AP/WIDE WORLD PHOTOS

A KIND OF MADNESS" is how a friend of mine, a Marine Corps veteran of the Vietnam War, described the courage displayed by men whose battlefield heroics had earned them the Medal of Honor. "It's impossible to comprehend, really, even if you witness it. . . . It's one mad moment. You never think anyone you know is really capable of it. Not even the toughest, bravest, best men in the company. They're as surprised as anyone to see it. And if someone does do it, and lives, they probably never do it again. You might think the guy who's always running around in a fight, exposing himself to enemy fire, yelling a lot, might do it. But that's not what happens. They just get killed usually."

Select at random a dozen Medal of Honor recipients and read the citations that accompany their decorations. Some will describe a single lonely act of heroism, one man's self-sacrifice that saved the lives of his comrades, who will remember the act for the rest of their lives with feelings of gratitude and lasting obligation mixed with something that feels much like shame—shame that one's life, no matter how good and useful, no matter how honorable, might not deserve to have been ransomed at such a cost. All the citations will record acts of great heroism, of course. But some might seem plausible, if just barely so. The reader might even fantasize himself capable of such heroism, under extreme circumstances, without feeling too ashamed of the presumption. Maybe you are. At least one, however, will tell of such incredible daring, such epic courage, that no witness to it could imagine himself, or anyone he knows, capable of it. It might be the story of Roy Benavidez.

Special Forces master sergeant Roy Benavidez was the son of a Texas sharecropper. Orphaned at a young age, quiet and mistaken as slow, derided as a "dumb Mexican" by his classmates, he left school in the eighth grade to work in the cotton fields. He joined the army at nineteen. On his first tour in Vietnam, in 1964, he stepped on a land mine. Army doctors thought the wound would be permanently crippling. It wasn't. He recovered and became a Green Beret.

During his second combat tour, in the early morning of May 2, 1968, in Loc Ninh, Vietnam, Sergeant Benavidez monitored by radio a twelve-man reconnaissance patrol. Three Green Berets, friends of his, and nine Montagnard tribesmen had been dropped in the dense jungle west of Loc Ninh, just inside Cambodia. No man aboard the low-flying helicopters beating noisily toward the landing zone that morning could have been unaware of how dangerous the assignment was. Considered an enemy sanctuary, the area was known to be vigilantly patrolled by a sizable force of the North Vietnamese army intent on keeping it so. Once on the ground, the twelve men were almost immediately engaged by the enemy and soon surrounded by a force that grew to a battalion.

The mission had been a mistake, and three helicopters were ordered to evacuate the besieged patrol. Fierce small arms and antiaircraft fire, wounding several crew members, forced the helicopters to return to base. Listening on the radio, Benavidez heard one of his friends scream, "Get us out of here!" and, "So much shooting it sounded like a popcorn machine." He jumped into one of the returning helicopters, volunteering for a second evacuation attempt. When he arrived at the scene, he found that none of the patrol had made it to the landing zone. Four were already dead, including the team leader, and the other eight were wounded and unable to move. Carrying a knife and a medic bag, Benavidez made the sign of the cross, leapt from the helicopter hovering ten feet off the ground, and ran seventy yards to his injured comrades. Before he reached them, he was shot in the leg, face, and head. He got up and kept moving.

When he reached their position, he armed himself with an enemy rifle, began to treat the wounded, reposition them, distribute ammunition, and call in air strikes. He threw smoke grenades to indicate their location and ordered the helicopter pilot to come in close to pick up the wounded. He dragged four of the wounded aboard, and then, while under intense fire and returning fire with his captured weapon, he ran alongside the helicopter as it flew just a few feet off the ground toward the others. He got the rest of the wounded aboard, as well as the dead, except for the fallen team leader. As he raced to retrieve his body, and the classified documents the dead man had carried, he was shot in the stomach and grenade fragments cut into his back.

Before he could make his way back toward the helicopter, the pilot was fatally wounded and the aircraft crashed upside down. He helped the wounded escape the burning wreckage and organized them in a defensive perimeter. He called for air strikes and fire from circling gunships to suppress the ever increasing enemy fire enough to allow another evacuation attempt. Critically wounded, Benavidez moved constantly along the perimeter, bringing water and ammunition to the defenders, treating their wounds, encouraging them to hold on. He sustained several more gunshot wounds, but he continued to fight. For six hours.

When another extraction helicopter landed, he helped the wounded toward it, one and two at a time. On his second trip, an enemy soldier ran up behind him and struck him with his rifle butt. Sergeant Benavidez turned to close with the man and his bayonet and fought him, hand to hand, to the death. Wounded again, he recovered the rest of his comrades. As the last were lifted onto the helicopter, he exchanged more gunfire with the enemy, killing two more Vietnamese soldiers, and then ran back to collect the classified documents before at last climbing aboard and collapsing, apparently dead.

The army doctor back at Loc Ninh thought him dead anyway. Bleeding profusely, his intestines spilling from his stomach wounds, completely immobile, and unable to speak, Benavidez was placed into a body bag. As the doctor began to pull up the black shroud's zipper, Roy Benavidez spit in his face. They flew him to Saigon for surgery, where he began a year in hospitals recovering from seven serious gunshot wounds, twenty-eight shrapnel wounds, and bayonet wounds in both arms.

Hard to believe, isn't it, what this one man did? And why? Because his buddies called out to him? Because the training just took over? Because it was automatic, he was in the moment, aware of what was required of him but senseless to the probable futility of his efforts? These are the sort of explanations you usually hear from someone who has distinguished himself in battle. They really don't help us understand. They mean something, but as an explanation for that kind of heroism, they are as unenlightening to me as haiku poetry. What kind of training prepares you to do that? What kind of unit solidarity, how great the love and trust for the man to your right and your left, inspires you to the superhuman heroics of Roy Benavidez?

I'll be damned if I know. I was trained to be an aviator, not a Special Forces commando. But how does anyone—Green Beret, navy SEAL, whatever—learn to be that brave? How do you build that kind of courage in someone? It certainly appears to be superhuman and incomprehensible to those with a more human-size supply, brave and resourceful though they may be. I can't explain it. No one I know can.

We are taught to understand, correctly, that courage is not the absence of fear, but the capacity for action despite our fears. Does anyone have that great a store of courage that he would think himself capable of meaningful action with the eruption of fear that any one of us would have felt rise in our throats and burn our hearts were we to find ourselves in the hopeless situation of Roy Benavidez? I wouldn't. I don't know anyone who would, and I've known some very brave men. I doubt very much Roy Benavidez thought he would. I would challenge the sanity of any reader who imagines the possibility of possessing such mastery over fear. It's not to be expected in anyone. No courage could contend with such fear, and animate our limbs, and control our minds. Fear would have to be vanquished completely.

Roy Benavidez jumped off the helicopter, acutely aware of the situation, perhaps, of the enemy's strength, of their location, of the circumstances of his comrades, of what needed to be done, but somehow insensate to the hopelessness of it all, to the gravity of his wounds, to the futility of fighting on. What pushed him? A tsunami of adrenaline? What carried him through? A sublime fatalism, driven by love or sense of duty to resign himself completely to the situation, whatever its horrors, and make his last hour his greatest? We can't know. All we can know is that in one moment of madness, six hours long, Roy Benavidez became to the men he saved, and maybe to himself, an avenging angel of God, masterful, indomitable, and utterly fearless.

If we can't comprehend his heroism or imagine possessing his courage, can it offer our own lives any instruction? I believe it can. Roy's life won't teach us how to save eight men while sustaining several dozen wounds. An act of heroism, of extraordinary courage, the grandeur of it, won't easily inspire us to act in imitation, but it can inspire us to emulate its author. For that, we should learn what we can of the whole experience of the subject, the hero's life, as it was before and after, and believe that trying to emulate the character it reveals is one tried way to prepare for the tests that might await us and gain hope that our courage will not be wanting in the moment.

We must accept the fact that some heroes, whether their courage was momentary or constant, might have led less than admirable lives. I don't think, however extraordinary the courage, that it will attain the grandeur of the inspirational to a sound mind were it motivated by selfish or malevolent purposes, or exercised by someone whose life, on the whole, was contemptible. Unless, of course, an act of heroism was an anomaly in the life that preceded it and character changing thereafter. The stories cherished most by all sinners whose consciences are not permanently mute concern the life-redeeming act of courage. They're not, however, as abundant in real life as they are in fiction. Better to look to the lives of good men and women who in a crucible risked or sacrificed their own security for someone else.

What do we know of Roy Benavidez's life before and after that moment of madness? We know that he was a good man. The straitened circumstances of his youth did not embitter him or lead him astray. The constant, lifelong pain of his wounds didn't undo him. His valor was not properly recognized for thirteen years. In 1981, Ronald Reagan—who said of his heroism that were it a movie script "you wouldn't believe it"—replaced the Distinguished Service Cross that General William Westmoreland had given Roy in 1968 with the Medal of Honor. The delay didn't seem to bother Roy. "I don't like to be called a hero," he complained, and then, in the familiar refrain of veterans from all wars, he offered the observation, "The real heroes are the ones who gave their lives for their country." That kind of humility from surviving veterans who distinguished themselves in combat is so commonplace that we've come to expect it from them. We don't take it seriously. We even suspect that it's false. We don't see how remarkable it is. They mean it. Every word.

Roy stayed in the army until he retired in 1976. Then he lived on his pension and disability pay and spent his time speaking at schools and to youth groups, counseling troubled kids, encouraging them to stay in school and off drugs. In 1998, on his deathbed, with two pieces of shrapnel still in his heart, he proclaimed: "I'm proud to be an American."

The navy named a ship after him and the army a building. His hometown erected a statue. But Hollywood never made a movie about him. No one would have believed it.

My LATE COLLEAGUE PAT MOYNIHAN coined the phrase *defining deviancy down* to criticize how American culture in the late twentieth century embraced situational morality in reaction to increasing rates of crime and other social ills rather than insist on the preservation of moral absolutes as the foundation of a functioning liberal society. America, he argued, evaded the hard choices such absolutes require and had, disastrously, learned to tolerate "much conduct previously stigmatized."

Similarly, American culture over the last thirty years or so has defined courage down. We have attributed courage to all manner of actions that may indeed be admirable but hardly compare to the conscious self-sacrifice on behalf of something greater than self-interest that once defined courage. We have come to identify one or more of the elements of courage—fortitude, discipline, daring, or righteousness, for example—as the entire virtue. Today, in our excessively psychoanalyzed society, sharing one's secret fears with others takes courage. So does escaping a failing marriage. So does "having it all," a career, children, and leisure. Refusing to help enable a loved one to indulge a ruinous vice is an act of courage. We say it takes courage to be different from the mainstream in our preferences in fashion, music, the length and color of our hair.

These are, of course, absurd examples of our profligate misidentification of the virtue of courage.

There are many other, closer calls. Is an athlete's prowess and guts on the field an example of courage? Is suffering illness or injury without complaint courageous? Is a sense of duty that withstands regular temptation but never encounters the possibility of really terrifying challenges? Is outspokenness in a culture of silent acquiescence to certain wrongs? Not always. They may be everyday behavior typical of courageous people. They may be evidence of virtuousness. They may be steps along the way to acquiring courage. But of themselves, these acts, admirable though they are, are not sufficient proof of courage.

If the standard for courage remains, as I think it should, acts that risk life or limb or other very serious personal injuries for the sake of others or to uphold a virtue—a standard often upheld by battlefield heroics but one that is certainly not limited to martial valor—these acts fall short of it by varying degrees. Yet they are celebrated as courageous by almost all of us today, and it seems stingy to consider them less so. But what are the consequences of generosity in defining courage? If a people believe that courage constitutes something less perilous, less dear, than the standard defined above, don't we risk having too few examples of real courage, grand courage, the kind that inspires a person and a society to reach beyond goodness to greatness? If children are taught that simply being honest or doing the best they can or appreciating what they have without complaint is considered by their society to be an act of courage, will they be more or less motivated to summon the real thing in a crucible? Will they take the hill in a

battle when no shame is attached—
on the contrary, when courage is as-
cribed—to holding one's ground,
if that were the best they could
do? Will they risk imprisonment or
some grave wrong to themselves to
defend a political principle if no less
courage is attributed to cherishing
the principle privately in safety?

Angela Dawson hated what
drug dealers were doing to Oliver,
her East Baltimore neighborhood.
Many of the families there were
fighting to maintain a decent quality
of life despite limited economic
means and the depravations that
surrounded them. Oliver is a place
where neat row houses, active
churches, and carefully tended play-
grounds line streets that were once
happy with the laughter of innocent
children. But now they called her
part of the neighborhood "the badlands." Many of the row houses had

been abandoned and boarded up, and some streets seemed paved with broken glass, crack vials, and bullet shells. Hard young men patrolled the streets, habitual criminals by their early teens, prowling for customers and on the lookout for cops and anyone who might disrupt their trade, the commerce of the desperate.

She was thirty-six years old, the mother of five children, who struggled not only to keep them safe in a culture of extreme violence, but to rise above despair and help them make something of themselves that would prove her values and courage superior to the cruelty and misery that an outside observer would have assumed were the natural state of their environment. She walked them to school, ate lunch with them, talked with their teachers, supervised their schoolwork, played with them, and kept their home as clean and comfortable as time and circumstances allowed.

She was a high school dropout who bore her first child at nineteen. Jobs were hard to find and keep. She and her husband fought sometimes, and their quarrels had become violent. Her husband had in the past sought to purchase a moment's tranquillity from the young men on street corners who peddled its illusion in small vials. They weren't saints. They made mistakes, let hardship get the better of them from time to time. But they didn't give up. She worked hard. Her husband worked hard. They persevered and fought to make their world a little more inhabitable. She had some kind of guts. She would not accept that people in her situation were consigned to violent and destitute lives. She complained when the commotion on the streets got to be too much to keep some semblance of order, when kids were fighting or breaking windows or playing music too loudly or when they were selling crack to one another and to the suburban types who came to the badlands in search of it. She refused to let the dealers ply their trade in front of her home and her children. She talked to them, yelled at them, threatened them, and called the police when they wouldn't take her seriously. Some of her neighbors, who admired her, thought she might have gone too far sometimes, pushed the dealers a little too hard, a little too publicly. She made them look bad, and that could get you in a lot of trouble in their neighborhood. They were right.

She didn't seem to care at first. She kept right after them even when some of them threw bricks through her windows as a warning that they had had enough of her crusade. But when an angry neighbor threw a couple of Molotov cocktails through her window, she began to fear the consequences of her actions. She reached a point where she was too afraid to take her kids to school. But still she refused to leave the neighborhood. She refused to give in and give up.

Then, at 2:18 on the morning of October 16, 2002, a twenty-one-year-old neighbor set Angela's house on fire, killing her, her husband, Carnell, and her five children. Before she perished, her neighbors heard her cry, "God, please help me. Help me get my children out."

It's hard not to wish, as some of her neighbors did, that Angela Dawson had had a little less courage. Isn't it better to give in to despair than die for your hope of a better life? Or worse yet, to see your children die for the sake of your aspirations for them? Maybe Angela felt that way too in the moment she realized that her courage would claim not only her life, but her children's lives as well. What parent wouldn't have surrendered to almost any iniquity to spare the life of his or her child? Popular culture usually conceives heroism, especially heroism that sacrifices the hero's life, as the ultimate in romantic gestures, the defiant last stand, one person alone against a host of evil. It almost seems a painless, welcome death. So far removed are they from our experience, these grand and inspiring legends, that we almost picture the hero as more than prepared, even happy to die with his virtue and courage intact. But then the composed nobility of the courageous act seems to get lost a little in the grim details that depict the sacrifice in its full horror, when we hear the mother's anguished appeal to God for her children's survival. All we can think about is how terrible and pointless and avoidable an end it was. We picture ourselves in the situation pleading for life, and we're somehow surprised to learn that heroes have to suffer the same agony. It confounds us. But why should it? Such are the wages of courage. Not for every act of courage, of course. Maybe not for most. But Angela Dawson wasn't the first person, nor will she be the last, to pay such a terrible price for her courage.

If you want to possess a true appreciation of courage, you must comprehend all its possible consequences in all their horror. They'll make you flinch. Certainly courage will lose some of its romantic quality. They might put you off the whole idea of it. But however uncomfortable we are made by the grisly and unimaginably heartbreaking details of such sacrifice, we should not feel less the nobility of it. On the contrary, despite the urge to avert your eyes from the suffering, the only way to really appreciate the nobility of courage is to familiarize yourself with its costs so that you will come to understand how rare a thing it really is.

As courage may demand such appalling sacrifice, so it demands economy in its definition. What person who heard Angela's last cry could ever again ascribe courage to someone who stuck with a diet or quit an unrewarding job or changed a hairstyle? It is no easy thing being truly brave. We should all know that before we presume we're ready for the experience of courage.

But we should know something else about courage. I wish Angela Dawson had had less of it or at least had employed her courage more subtly and less boldly. I wish her killer had had some small measure of humanity left alive in his heart. I wish Baltimore and the whole country would find a way to make every neighborhood in America safe and livable so that people like Angela wouldn't take the risks she did. I wish her children had survived. But I also wish I had half her courage. "Courage is like love," Napoleon said. "It must have hope to nourish it." And hope in the measure that fueled Angela Dawson's courage must be a hell of a powerful thing, a life-transforming thing.

In our culture it is very unlikely that many of our children would ever face such crucibles. We are a strong, mostly lawful, prosperous country. Our frontier has long been conquered. Many of the most dread diseases have been eradicated or made treatable. The core political values of our free society are so deeply embedded in our collective consciousness that only a few malcontents from the most extreme political fringes, lunatics generally, ever dare to threaten them. Crime rates rise and fall and rise again, and claim victims and leave tragedies behind, but lawlessness is still much less prevalent today than it was a century ago. We are the world's only superpower, with armed forces so powerful that they deter all but the most irrational of adversaries from significantly challenging our security. We don't have as much to fear as we had in the past. Courage may be in scarce supply, but the demand appears down as well. And we have come to grade courage on the curve.

It is surely a good thing that parents can tuck their children into bed at night with a fair amount of confidence that they will grow up safe and sound, free to pursue their dreams with only the remote possibility that some truly terrifying challenge will block their path. It's a very good thing, indeed, a society that many generations labored mightily to create. But the accomplishment could very well have made it harder to help build in a child the kind of courage that made it all possible when the occasions for proving such courage are ever decreasing, when courage doesn't really seem necessary very often.

Approximately two hundred thousand Americans went to Iraq to destroy the regime of Saddam Hussein. From a country of 270 million, that is less than 1 percent of the population. And of those who went, an even smaller number actually participated in combat.

So removed from our own experience has such action become that we, like the enemy, witnessed their might and their heroism, as we sat snugly in our family rooms staring at the television, with something akin to shock and awe and, let's be honest, a thrilling pleasure to see our country's armed forces so fearsome, so peerlessly powerful. But it wasn't all pleasure. We felt for every casualty, as we should have. We anguished over every captured or missing soldier, gasped at the images of children harmed unintentionally by our bombs and bullets, exulted in the speed with which the enemy collapsed lest a day's delay cause one other American family to suffer a loss, as well we should have. When those brave men and women returned, we celebrated their triumph and courage, our pride at their achievement coinciding with our tremendous relief over their return. We should be proud of them. They deserve it.

Although the guerrilla war that followed in its aftermath has proved tougher and lasted longer than expected, the destruction of Saddam's armed forces was quick and decisive. The enemy was vastly overmatched. But the cause was just, and I believe necessary, and our soldiers fought as bravely and as competently and as humanely as they were asked. They earned their honor. Their heroism was no less distinguished because they enjoyed an overwhelming advantage in high-tech weaponry. In the marshes south of Baghdad, marines were ordered to "fix bayonets" to fight visiting terrorists from Syria, Lebanon, and other countries. To face the enemy at close quarters is an extremely courageous thing, a hard thing to imagine in a society that has little experience of war.

Thrilling, mesmerizing, shocking, frightening, but was it unforgettable? Will we remember? We should. Those who gave their lives in service to their country deserve to be remembered. Should, as we hope and intend, another people in a country far from ours gain and keep their own right to self-determination, that would be an accomplishment worth remembering. But will it? I wonder. The thrill of it will fade away. We're a society quite familiar with thrills. We constantly seek new ones, and the shelf life of their effect contracts correspondingly. What will remain in our national memory? Will we attempt to inspire our own courage some distant day by recalling the heroics of our compatriots in Iraq?

Hᴏᴡ ᴍᴀɴʏ ᴀᴍᴇʀɪᴄᴀɴꜱ ꜱᴛɪʟʟ remember the Battle of Peleliu Island? Not many, I suspect. I didn't remember it in any detail before a recent trip to the Palaus, the coral island archipelago in the western Pacific where Peleliu lies near the southern end. Overshadowed by events in the European theater and MacArthur's return to the Philippines, Peleliu, a speck of land only eight miles long and three miles across at its widest, where prodigious blood was shed in a possibly unnecessary battle late in World War II, has never enjoyed an exalted place in the history of Pacific theater battles. Its details are probably forgotten to all but the professional

Marines advance on Peleliu Island, 1944.

CORBIS

or avid amateur historian. That's a pity. The corps commander there called it the "toughest fight of the war." Eugene Sledge, a twenty-one-year-old private in the legendary First Marine Division, fought at Peleliu and wrote movingly of the experience that haunted him for years. He remembered it as a "netherworld of horror," where "time had no meaning; life had no meaning. The fierce struggle made savages of us all."

When the marines of the First Division swarmed the beaches of Peleliu, they were prepared for a tough but very quick fight with the island's Japanese defenders. The division commander, Major General William Rupertus, had told them the battle would be "rough, but fast." Intelligence reports had not detected a sizable enemy force or heavy fortifications and had de-

scribed a "mostly low and flat terrain." Earlier engagements with the
enemy had taught the marines to
expect a fierce and terrifying assault
on their beachhead by suicide waves
of Japanese attackers. It would be, as
such experiences were, a hellish few
days, Rupertus thought, but just a
few days at the most. As it turned
out, the Battle of Peleliu would last
more than ten weeks. A garrison of
more than ten thousand Japanese
soldiers and conscripted laborers,
who had been preparing six months
for the battle they knew would
come, would fight to the death.

Operation Stalemate II had been
conceived to protect MacArthur's
flank in his final drive to retake
the Philippines. Two days before
the operation, Admiral Bull Halsey
recommended to Admiral Chester
Nimitz that the invasion be called
off. His Fifth Fleet had been suc-

cessfully attacking Japanese bases in the Palaus and the Philippines for weeks and meeting with lighter than anticipated resistance. He concluded that the Japanese defense of the Philippines wouldn't be as formidable as war planners had assumed; that the timetable for the invasion of Leyte Island should be accelerated; and that an invasion of Peleliu, to secure an air base there, wouldn't be necessary to protect the attack on Leyte. Nimitz cabled the Joint Chiefs of Staff, who then conferred with President Roosevelt and General MacArthur, who decided to accept part of Halsey's recommendation. The invasion of Leyte would be advanced two months, and the second phase of Operation Stalemate II would be dropped. The invasion of Peleliu, along with two other islands in the archipelago,

Ulithi and Angaur, would proceed as planned.

D-day was September 15, 1944. Three days of naval bombardments preceded the invasion, until, as one officer mistakenly believed, they had "run out of targets." The first of three regiments, the First Marines, under the command of Marine Corps legend Colonel Lewis "Chesty" Puller, hit the western beaches of Peleliu at 8:30 that morning. The Fifth and Seventh Marines followed right behind, all three regiments fighting abreast along a two-mile front. There were experienced veterans among the assault forces, but the bulk of the men landing that day were teenagers, straight out of boot camp.

The Japanese had changed their tactics, learning from experience that banzai suicide attacks resulted in quick defeats. On Peleliu they planned a protracted struggle, small unit counterattacks, a war of attrition from hidden defenses, mindful that the Americans would eventually overcome them but determined to exact for as long as they could a very high price for their defeat. The Japanese resisted the landings ferociously; their artillery destroyed dozens of the marines' amphibious tractors (amtracs). Enfilading fire from the high coral ridges above the beaches, particularly one nicknamed "the Point," cut down hundreds of marines in the first hours of the invasion. Counterattacking Japanese soldiers, exploiting holes in the American lines, infiltrated marine companies isolated from the main assault force. But the enemy's only major attack, a combined tank and infantry attack at 4:30 that afternoon, was a disaster. The marines'

Sherman tanks destroyed the attacking force in detail.

That was the only time the Japanese attacked in the open. All other counterattacks were smaller, better concealed, and effective. A witness estimated that throughout the first day and night of the invasion, one marine was killed or wounded every two and a half minutes. Chesty Puller's regiment caught the worst of it, facing the fiercest resistance on the assault's left flank and reporting more than five hundred men killed or wounded in the first twenty-four hours. The marines fought all night from their foxholes and the next day resumed their advance, as the Japanese fell back to their final defensive positions in hundreds of caves and concrete bunkers hidden amid a series of craggy limestone ridges, a formidable redoubt in the center of the island named the Umurbrogal Mountain.

Temperatures rose to 115 degrees and higher through-out the first week. Drinking water was scarce, and food provisions were depleted. Monsoon rains, while bringing some relief to the sweltering marines, turned battlegrounds into muddy swamps. Hacking their way through thick jungles and mangrove swamps, braving cannon and machine-gun fire to seize one ridge after another (in some instances they were driven from heights they had struggled heroically to take and forced to fight for them all over again), the marines were taking horrific casualties to sustain their advance. The division commander, General Rupertus, still believing that the invasion could be brought to a swift conclusion and determined to prevent the army from reinforcing and claiming a share of the victory, repeatedly ordered his regimental commanders to make frontal assaults on fortified enemy positions until they were exhausted, their ranks so decimated that some battalions were incapable of effective action. By the sixth day, Puller's regiment had suffered more than 1,700 casualties.

The corps commander, Major General Roy Geiger, visited the First Marines and saw for himself their condition. Over the loud objections of the foolhardy Rupertus, Geiger ordered that the regiment be evacuated and the army's 81st Infantry Division and 321st Regimental Combat Team, then engaged in mopping up operations on a nearby island, replace them. By the time they were relieved, the First Marines had killed almost four thousand of the enemy, nearly a quarter of the garrison, and taken the Point, ten other coral ridges, and nearly two hundred heavily defended caves, Japanese blockhouses, and pillboxes.

The fight for Peleliu would go on for more than two months after that first savage week. It is hard to do justice to the suffering there. No man having experienced it would ever forget it. Many of the marines who fought there would fight in other campaigns, notably in the bloody struggle to take Okinawa. None of them believed they ever had it worse than their first days and weeks on Peleliu.

The Japanese fought almost to the last man. The job of digging them out of the caves of Umurbrogal Mountain was mostly the army's. They did it one cave and bunker at a time, with flamethrowers mounted on amtracs and by dynamiting and bulldozing the caves into crypts, sealing the enemy inside to starve to death. Of the estimated 10,900 defenders, only a few dozen, most of them conscripted workers, surrendered in November. Even then a few stragglers continued to fight on. The cost of the campaign to the Americans was not as huge, but it was staggering nevertheless. The marines took seven thousand casualties, the army fourteen hundred. The first battles for the Philippines, the advance Peleliu was intended to protect, had begun at Leyte Island in October. U.S. bombers wouldn't begin flying out of bases in the Palaus to support operations in the Philippines for more than a month after the campaign had begun. Without ships or aircraft, the Japanese presence in the Palaus had never really been a threat to MacArthur's famous promise.

But the pointlessness of the sacrifice on Peleliu certainly doesn't diminish the heroism with which it was made.

Should we care that the battle of Peleliu has been, by and large, forgotten by the descendants of the men who fought there, the fortunate beneficiaries of their courage? It seems ungrateful of us, obviously, but that's not so unusual, is it? Children rarely appreciate fully the sacrifices their parents make, no matter how much we remind them. That's human nature. And it's a very different world now from what it was then. Our children are safe enough to think wars aren't really big things anymore. And thank God for that. Science, medicine, technology, commerce—those are their big things. Wars are impressive. But they're usually over pretty quickly, and we don't really notice much of a change when they're finished. Perhaps some people do, but the rest of us are too busy with our big things. Peleliu was a big thing— sixty years ago. The men who fought there were tougher than us. So what? How is that relevant to the problems we have to work on today?

Courage on the scale manifested in Peleliu—hard held, impossibly enduring, selfless, true in all its bloodstained, filthy, aching grandeur, summoned every day for months—will almost surely never be known or needed by us personally. Wars aren't fought that way anymore. Few of us will fight in any kind of war. There's not much chance of truly big, historically important political conflict in this country, either. What do politicians fight about anymore? The size of tax cuts. What to spend our money on. These are the most common areas of domestic policy disagreements. We're all pretty much agreed on the big question—whether man is endowed by his Creator with certain inalienable rights and that just government is derived from the consent of the governed. What do we need so much courage for?

THE IDEA FOR THIS BOOK came from our creative editor, Jon Karp. He thought I might have something useful to say in an essay on courage. The concept began to germinate in his imagination in the weeks after September 11, when people were afraid to ride elevators to the higher floors of tall buildings or get on airplanes, when many thought their entire sense of well-being had been permanently compromised. He thought I could encourage people to find the fortitude to get on with their lives by writing a manual of courage, so to speak. Several talk show hosts in the weeks just after September 11 also thought I might possess such insights. They're wrong. I'm not trained in psychoanalysis. I don't know what to tell people to quiet those kinds of anxieties. Get on the damn elevator! Fly on the damn plane! Calculate the odds of being harmed by a terrorist! It's still about as likely as being swept out to sea by a tidal wave. Watch the terrorist alert and go outside again when it falls below yellow. Suck it up, for crying out loud. You're almost certainly going to be okay. And in the unlikely event you're not, do you really want to spend your last days cowering behind plastic sheets and duct tape? That's not a life worth living, is it?

Please don't think I dismiss the importance of what happened on that terrible morning in September. I don't. Beyond the immeasurable grief and suffering it brought to thousands of American families, it was a battle cry that summoned America to a war we sort of knew was going on, but we hadn't really comprehended how near the threat was and how atrocious were the purposes and plans of our enemy. It is a big thing, this war, a fight between two ideologies completely antithetical to each other. It's a fight between a just regard for human dignity and a malevolent force that defiles an honorable religion by disputing God's love for every soul on earth. It's a fight between right and wrong, good and evil. It is no more ambiguous than that. And should the enemy acquire for their arsenal the chemical, biological, and nuclear weapons they seek, this war will become an even bigger thing. It will become a fight for survival. It certainly warrants our courage.

However, most of us will not need to fight in this war, not in the conventional sense of fighting. There will be armed conflict, as there already has been in Afghanistan and Iraq. But for the most part, the enemy will not be confronted in conventional battles, massed armies squaring off in the desert sun. Much of it will be fought by intelligence services, with our enemies killed a few at a time by HARM missiles fired from drones or at the hands of our Special Forces. Much of it will be fought politically, diplomatically, economically. And even if it requires further armed conflict as in Afghanistan and Iraq, few of us will be needed to bear arms.

The majority of us will stay at home, going about our business with or without a heightened sense of alertness, keeping the old home fires burning, the economy functioning, and, we hope, our morale up. It would be an admirable thing if we honored our compatriots' sacrifice and our country's cause by showing our patriotism in more than symbolic ways, by joining in some form of national service. Some of us not plagued by advanced years could consider enlisting in one of the services. Last time I checked, the recruitment rolls weren't full. But it won't be necessary for most of us to do so. So believe in our country, love our founding truths, honor the sacrifice of our soldiers, be a good citizen, and fly on the damn airplane. That's all I can offer in the way of instruction to people who might feel incapacitated by the threat of terrorism. And it makes for a very short book.

However, I think I can offer a few more thoughts about courage. Not because I possess such an ample store of it myself. I wish I did. But I have spent time in the company of heroes. I was raised by them, served with them, was taught to revere them through instruction in the tradition of martial courage. I know what courage looks like. I know what it can do. I know its different expressions. I think I know what it costs. And if I can't tell you how to get Roy Benavidez's courage—no one could, not even Roy—I can provide a few suggestions, learned by observing the example of the people I admire the most, about what one might do, how one might live, to become ready for the occasion of heroism and possibly, in a difficult, dark, confused, and consequential moment, to strike what an old soldier's prayer hails the "little spark of courage."

First we must answer the question "So what?" What do we need courage for anymore? Not to quiet our anxieties caused by September 11. A sense of proportion and a little righteous anger ought to suffice for that job. So what do we need it for?

We need it because without courage all virtue is fragile: admired, sought, professed, but held cheaply and surrendered without a fight. Courage is what Winston Churchill called "the first of human qualities . . . because it guarantees all the others." That's what we mean by the courage of our convictions. Not that our convictions possess an innate courage, but that if we lack the courage to hold them, not just when they accord with the convictions of others but against threatening opposition, in the moment of their testing, they're superficial, vain things that add nothing to our self-respect or our society's respect for the virtues we profess. We can admire virtue and abhor corruption sincerely, but without courage we are corruptible.

I once heard a story about the late University of Alabama football coach Bear Bryant, possibly apocryphal, but it has stuck with me. Before the start of every game, Bryant would walk his quarterback along the sidelines in silence for all but a moment of the ritual, the moment when he would turn to the young athlete and give him just two words of advice: "Be brave." It's pretty obvious why that would be good advice to a quarterback. Be brave, because as you're coiled behind the center ready to take the snap, you're going to be looking into the determined faces of several men, larger, stronger, and probably tougher than you, grunting oaths to do you grievous bodily harm. And when you touch the ball, they're going to have one thing on their minds: to slam your body to the hard ground. And if they crush your bones in the process, that would be just fine, too. You're going to feel a strong urge to protect yourself, to not trust your line, the ability of your receivers to get open, your skill at slipping the monster's grasp while watching downfield for the moment when you must stop evading the tackle, bring up your arm, fire the ball spiraling toward its target, and then, because your charging opponents might be too close to brake their forward momentum, take the hit and get back up. You're going to want to run away from the probability of pain and not worry about completing the play. During the course of a game, Bear Bryant would have issued a hundred instructions to his quarterback. None of them could have been as important as his first. Be brave.

It doesn't matter how athletic you are, how strong, how swift, how accurate your arm, how good your instincts—without the courage to exercise your talents when pressed by formidable opposition, they're useless. Without courage you're not a quarterback at all.

Fewer of us will be college or professional quarterbacks than will go to war. Physical courage would be nice, we might think. We could relieve the boredom of our tame recreations by taking up more adventurous pursuits like hang gliding or mountain climbing. How exciting can golf be when we could be skydiving? It would be great to have the guts for it. But golf will do if we don't have the heart for something more thrilling, and the quality of

Paul W. "Bear" Bryant, 1957

our lives won't suffer much. The need for courage, physical courage, we might wrongly conclude, doesn't really exist for most of us. Maybe it's just a thing of vanity for all but the soldier, the fireman, and the cop. Maybe we just feel a need to prove our courage to attract the admiration of others.

Most of us see the need for moral courage. Most of us accept social norms: that it's right to be honest, to respect the rights of others, to have compassion. But accepting the appropriateness of these qualities, wanting them, and teaching our children to want them aren't the same as actually possessing them. Accepting their validity isn't moral courage. How honest are we if we tell the truth most of the time and stay silent only when telling the truth might get us fired or earn us a broken nose? We need moral courage to be honest all the time. It's the enforcing virtue, the one that makes all the others possible. And it really isn't different from physical courage, except sometimes in degree and sometimes in the occasions when it encounters risk. If you don't have the courage to keep your virtue when facing unwanted consequences, you're not virtuous. You're not a quarterback at all.

If admiring and wanting virtue isn't virtuous, what is it? It's a start.

It is love that makes us willing to sacrifice, love that gives us courage. It moves the parent to rush into the burning house to save a child. But love often begins with desire. If we desire virtue strongly enough, we may come to love it. And if we love virtue so much that we consider the condition of not possessing it far more terrible than the consequences of keeping it, we must find the courage to hold it, however high the cost.

Parents who want their children to have courage usually think of it in its physical expression first and they try to impart it to them by experience and encouragement. When they fall from the horse we've set them upon, we'll encourage them to get back in the saddle. Don't be afraid of the ball, we tell them, trust your reflexes and your glove. Don't give up, keep trying, you'll get better. These are, of course, sensible encouragements to a child. They need to be so encouraged. But we're not exactly teaching them courage. We're teaching them physical skills. We're teaching them to be strong. We're helping them acquire fortitude. We're building their confidence and giving them hope. These are elements of courage in most instances, but not the whole virtue. Their effect alone might only be to give them daring, nerve. They might grow up and climb mountains or become risk-taking entrepreneurs. Not necessarily bad things. But is that all we think courage is? Is that what we're trying to teach them? Without other instruction, they could turn out to be Enron executives. They had daring, to be sure. But they lacked ethics. They lacked a sense of honor, and they lacked courage.

When I first began to think about what kind of guidance one could offer someone who wanted to find courage, an old joke about a get-rich scheme popular some forty or more years ago kept coming to mind. Back then you often saw matchbook covers suggest the secret of acquiring great wealth. "How to become a millionaire," they enticed. Then on the inside of the cover you found an address where you could write and in return for a small fee receive instructions on how to join the ranks of the privileged. The joke went that when you received the promised revelation, all it said was "First, get yourself a million dollars."

There you have it. The formula for becoming courageous: First, get yourself some courage. The rest is easy.

Although the advice might seem incomplete, you can't dismiss it as false. It's not that simple, obviously. But don't we usually think of courage simply in terms of whether we have it or not? How often do we really reflect on what we could do that might build our courage? Can you recall times when you've come home at the end of the day and fantasized about how you wished you had responded to the school bully or your abusive boss? That's usually an indicator that whatever qualities you possess, courage might not be among them. I've always worried that those are the experiences that flash before you in life's last moments—the regretted lost chances when you wished you had had courage. We think about what we would do with courage, not how to get it. It's easier. But if we spent more time searching for our courage and less time imagining the changes it might work in our personalities, we would probably die with fewer regrets.

How should we think about it? Are there habits, exercises, to gaining courage that we could try? Is it like losing weight? Should we hit the gym more often, toughen up, become stronger? Would that make us braver? It could be that increasing one's confidence can increase the possibility of courage. To the extent that enhancing your physical strength gives you more confidence, it might make you a little more daring, which in turn might—I stress might—in some small way encourage you to be a bit braver. However, I've known any number of physically fit cowards. I've known any number of self-assured cowards. And I've known quite a few humble, physically delicate people who had a lion's courage when they needed it.

Confidence surely plays some role in building our courage. But more than our physical attributes, I think it's a familiarity with fear and inhibitions and learning that we can act in spite of them that build the kind of confidence that can give us courage.

Biographies of Eleanor Roosevelt describe a woman who suffered from lifelong feelings of insecurity. Dowdy, retiring, self-effacing, she didn't give the physical impression or exhibit the personality that most of us associate with people who have courage. But she did have strength. She managed to act on her convictions in spite of her inhibitions. And if the fears she withstood were not akin to the terror of death faced on the battlefield, she still had to struggle all her life to resist their urgings, from letting them shut her into a life of comfortable seclusion from the kinds of encounters that frightened her. If not courage, she certainly had resolve, which is, I think, an approximation of the first virtue and can serve to induce courage. And she had some pretty good advice for people who, like her, suffered from potentially incapacitating anxieties.

"You gain strength, courage, and

confidence by every experience in which you really stop to look fear in the face. You are able to say to yourself, 'I lived through this horror. I can take the next thing that comes along.' ... You must do the thing you think you cannot do."

Do the thing you think you cannot do. Though it is as apparent and as insufficient an explanation of how we obtain courage as is the aforementioned prescription for becoming a millionaire, that doesn't make it useless advice. Eleanor Roosevelt managed to live an exceptionally useful life by following the prescription, useful to her and to many others, burdened though she was by her insecurities and doubts. Again, maybe her resolve wasn't exactly as empowering a condition as courage, but what more do most of us need courage for than to live life accord-

Eleanor Roosevelt at the Democratic convention in Chicago, July 19, 1940.

BETTMANN/CORBIS

ing to the dictates of our conscience?

Still, you might respond, you
don't need to be told to do things
you fear doing. You want to be told
how to do them. Well, I can't tell
you exactly. Neither could Eleanor.
You need to want to do them, of
course. But most of us do. Mrs.
Roosevelt advises that it's far more
important to need to have courage
than to want to have it. Needing
courage won't guarantee a constant
supply of the virtue, but putting
ourselves in situations that demand
our courage will more likely stir it
than daydreaming about it.

My father and his father believed
the best definition of courage was
Admiral Lord Nelson's advice: "No
captain can do very wrong if he
places his ship alongside that of the
enemy." It was the creed shared by
most of their navy peers, the men

they admired most. My grandfather's friend and commander, the rash and brave warrior Bull Halsey, called it his constant guide. "All problems, personal, national, or combat, become smaller if you don't dodge them. Touch a thistle timidly and it pricks you; grasp it boldly and its spines crumble. Carry the battle to the enemy. Lay your ship alongside his." It's an exhortation to charge toward the occasion of heroism, and somehow the very boldness of the act, the necessity of courage it imposes, will give you the courage to see the thing through. They believed their own experiences proved it true. They had sought every occasion to lay their ship alongside the enemy's and had never found their courage wanting when they did.

For many years I too believed it, that all you ever needed to do to gain courage was simply provoke it. I've seen it work. But eventually I discovered that courage wouldn't appear automatically every time you put yourself in need of it. Often it would, but it could soon exhaust itself. In prison, I would use my anger to prime the pump of my courage and provoke confrontations with the enemy. But many times, when I was weary and somewhat forlorn, I just couldn't recover the strength to put myself in need of it. I would hear the guard's keys jangling in his hand, coming my way, and I didn't want to lay my ship alongside his. I just wanted to take my ship to some safe, snug harbor that the enemy would never visit. I might have felt the tug of shame a little on those occasions, but you just got tired sometimes.

For a brief period, I lived in a cell next to one of our senior-ranking officers, a fierce resister, maybe the bravest of us all. The stories of what he would do to resist, to confront his enemies, were legends in the camp that greatly strengthened our morale and courage. Many times when I was brought back to my cell after an extended and physically challenging interrogation, the first thing I would do is tap on the wall to my neighbor, not just to communicate my most recent experience, but to show I could still defy our enemy. Communicating with my neighbors is usually what had landed me in the interrogation room in the first place.

Once, when my neighbor, the legendary resister, was hauled back into his cell after what appeared to be a pretty rough interrogation, I waited for him to tap me up on the wall so I could learn what had happened and offer him some encouragement, as he had so often given us. The tap never came. So I tried tapping him up again and then again. No reply ever came. He was as brave as they come, a good and great man. Sometimes you just get tired.

So if making our courage necessary isn't a fail-safe way of acquiring it, what is? Nothing. There are no guarantees of courage. Ever. We can only increase the probability of it. By wanting it, needing it, and wanting and needing those things it takes courage to obtain.

THINK OF THE BOLD ADVEN-
turers, the famous explorers of the
past. What personality trait comes
to mind other than their courage?
Isn't it curiosity? Don't we see them
as people driven by something close
to an insatiable need to know something not known? And the answers
they needed took courage to find.

We're all born inquisitive. Every
parent has experienced seemingly
ceaseless interrogation by children
seeking knowledge of all manner
of natural phenomena and human
history. Our intelligence develops
through inquiry. So, too, can our
curiosity help develop our courage
if we are fortunate at a young age
to be under the care of adults who

don't just patiently suffer our incessant demands for explanations of the world around us, but actively encourage our natural inquisitiveness. And curiosity can encourage our determination to find answers for ourselves through exploration, study, and testing when we do not get them from the human encyclopedia we assume our parents to be.

"Big George" Crookham was a curious old man. A farmer and salt boiler by trade, a self-taught natural scientist by avocation, he rambled through the fields and woods of Jackson County, Ohio, always on the lookout for another animal, bird, plant, or mineral to add to his extensive collection of specimens. In 1838, he befriended the family of Joseph Powell, an itinerant Welsh-born farmer and Methodist preacher, who had abandoned their homestead in upstate New York

John Wesley Powell

CORBIS

for what they hoped would be greater opportunity in Ohio and greater acceptance of their antislavery convictions. They were disappointed. Their new friend, George Crookham, was a fellow abolitionist, but he and they were a minority in Jackson County. The growing unrest between pro- and antislavery forces that divided neighbor from neighbor in many of the new settlements west of the Alleghenies had not spared the communities of southern Ohio. The Powells, especially the Powell children, were forced to suffer petty cruelties at the hands of neighbors, few of whom were slaveholders themselves but who, unlike the Powells and George Crookham, rejected the notion that God didn't distinguish between His black and white creations in the assignment of their natural rights.

The Powell boys, John Wesley

and Walter, were constantly taunted and physically abused by their schoolmates. On one occasion, they were stoned by other children on Main Street in the center of the village of Jackson while their assailants' proslavery parents applauded. Fearing for John Wesley's safety, Joseph removed him from the village school and placed him under the tutelage of George Crookham. In addition to his collection of natural specimens, Crookham possessed an ample library, as well as a laboratory where he tended his deep interest in the local geology, flora, and fauna. And he offered to share his knowledge with any young man who shared his passion for discovery. John Wesley was his prize pupil. For the next four years, teacher and student were rarely separated.

Crookham's teaching method concentrated on learning nature

firsthand, and his classroom was the outdoors. Taking John Wesley by the hand, he roamed the country-side in pursuit of new specimens, developing not only the boy's inter-est in natural history, but his self-reliance as well. Crookham took care not to restrict his instruction to the rote memorization of facts, but to encourage young Powell to learn what questions to ask of nature and what methods of inquiry would best yield the right answers. He was rewarded for his efforts by John Wesley's own prodigious intellectual curiosity and eagerness and the re-sourcefulness the boy employed in pursuit of knowledge.

In 1846, a proslavery mob burned George Crookham's school, destroying his collections and li-brary. Not long after, Joseph Powell moved his family to more politically sympathetic communities, first in

Wisconsin and then in northern Illinois. But the curious old man had left a permanent mark on his pupil, who parted from his teacher a more learned young man and, most important, a devoted natural historian with an almost aching need to understand the world around him.

His father wanted him to become a minister, but Powell had no intention of joining his father's profession. He attended school sporadically, but like his mentor he was an avid self-teacher. He traveled the waterways of the Midwest, collecting specimens, descending the Mississippi, Ohio, and Illinois rivers alone in a rowboat. For seven years he taught school in order to earn enough money to pursue his own education. He took courses at several local colleges. By his early twenties, he had earned sufficient reputation as a scholar and scientist to join the new

Illinois Natural History Society, becoming the curator of its conchology department, and to become superintendent of schools in Hennepin, Illinois.

By the election of Abraham Lincoln in 1860, civil war appeared inevitable. So Powell began a quick but thorough study of military science and engineering before enlisting as a private in the Twentieth Illinois Infantry Regiment. The regiment immediately elected him its sergeant major. By the time Twentieth Illinois was mustered into federal service in June 1861 and deployed to Cape Girardeau, Missouri, near St. Louis, Powell was commissioned a second lieutenant under the command of General Ulysses S. Grant. Grant ordered him to fortify the town and authorized him to recruit and train a battery company, which he did with his customary efficiency and dispatch. He was rewarded with promotion to captain of Battery F, Second Illinois Artillery, a short leave to marry his cousin, Emma Dean, and Grant's permission to bring his bride back to camp with him.

Shiloh was his first major battle. It was one of the bloodiest fights of the war, an important Union victory that had lasting consequences for the young artillery captain. As Powell raised his right arm to command another volley of cannon fire, a Confederate minié ball shattered his wrist and tore through his forearm. After briefly examining the wound, Union doctors decided to amputate his arm. Following a short recovery, his stump barely healed, Powell decided to stay in the army on condition that his wife remain at his side. He fought at the siege of Vicksburg, "the forty hardest days of my life," he later recalled, and marched on Atlanta. He remained on active duty until the last days of the war despite complications from his wound at Shiloh that necessitated another, painful operation. He retired with the rank of major, a title he expected others to address him by for the remainder of his life.

After the war, he accepted a position as professor of geology at Illinois Wesleyan University, and the following year the Illinois State Legislature appointed him curator of the newly endowed Illinois State Natural History Society. As a teacher, Powell copied the methods of his beloved mentor, George Crookham. He taught his students in the field, encouraging their fascination with nature and counseling them to examine life and think for themselves about its laws and history. He organized summer expeditions to the West, taking his students and the redoubtable and well-traveled Mrs. Powell to the Rocky Mountains. They traveled across the plains by wagon and horseback, climbed some of the tallest peaks in Colorado, including Pikes Peak, which Emma Powell was the first woman to ascend. When most of the party returned to Illinois in September, the Powells and a few others remained behind to explore the remote headwaters of the Grand River, as the upper reaches of the Colorado were then called.

He led a second expedition the following summer, with the intention of collecting geological and geographic information through the winter. After the party built winter quarters on the White River, Powell left them to explore on his own. Carrying several scientific instruments and few other provisions, unarmed in a wilderness inhabited by little-known Indian tribes, Powell traveled south to the Grand River, then down the White and Green rivers, and then north to the Uinta Mountains.

He spent much of the winter with the White River Utes, beginning his lifelong interest in, and respect and empathy for the native peoples of North America. He learned their language, compiled a rough dictionary of their vocabulary, and studied their history and customs. His experiences that first winter, and subsequent similar experiences with Navajo, Hopi, Paiute, and Shivwit tribes, taught him a great appreciation for the ways and values of Indians. He was fascinated by their language and customs and believed they had the same right to live according to their traditions as he had to live by his. His hosts returned his respect in kind. In his many years traveling among them, years before the tribes of the Southwest were forced onto reservations by the inexorable progress of white settlement, Powell never felt compelled to carry a weapon. He felt then, and felt for the rest of his life, that he was among friends in their company. He had an Indian name, given to him by the White River Utes—Kapurats, "One Arm Off"—and in all the camps and villages of the many tribes he would later visit, he would discover that his name had preceded him.

It was during this first winter expedition that Powell decided on his greatest adventure. The Colorado was the most unknown and forbidding river in the American West. No explorer had charted or knew its course. One man who had explored its waters south of the canyon predicted that the Colorado, "along with the greater part of its lonely and majestic way," would be "forever unvisited and undisturbed." But after studying the course of its tributary rivers, and with knowledge gained from talking to Indians and mountain men familiar with the region, Powell theorized that the river preceded the wild, unexplored wilderness of the Grand Canyon and then cut through it as the canyon's walls rose to their towering majesty. He believed the Colorado could be descended by small boat through the Grand Canyon to its western terminus, and he intended to test his hypothesis the following summer.

"Is any other nation so ignorant of itself?" Powell asked as he sought financial backing for his plan. He would explore the last unknown wilderness of the continental United

States to remove that charge against his country's reputation and for the sake of an answer to a simple question: What was there? He was not an adventurer, who traveled simply for the thrill of the journey. His purpose was discovery. He was a scientist, with a scientist's faith in his profession's indispensability to the progress of mankind.

On May 24, 1869, with personal, private, and limited public funds, permission to requisition supplies from army depots, and four small boats built in Chicago to his specifications, Powell, his brother, Walter, and eight other men—an army sergeant, five mountain men, an unemployed local teenager, and an English adventurer—none of whom had any experience navigating white water, embarked from a little railroad station in Wyoming Territory on the first leg of their journey. They would descend the Green River to its confluence with the Colorado and then follow the mysterious river to the end. No human being had ever done it, not even the Indians who lived in or near the Grand Canyon, who believed the canyon gorge to be impervious to human navigation. Many among the small crowd watching the expedition launch believed they had seen the last of the intrepid crew. Smart money would have bet on it.

The Colorado River Exploring Expedition had adequate provisions for the journey, but their boats, described by a writer as resembling "walnut shells," were unsuited for the hazards of navigating the whitewater rapids that coursed between them and their destination. Neither Powell, who designed them, nor the boatwrights who built them had ever run rapids before, and their ignorance produced boats that were sound only in calm water. Calamity struck only sixteen days and 150 miles into their thousand-mile journey. After safely running the first canyons, falls, and rapids of their voyage, the party approached Lodore Canyon, where rising waters, roiling in channels strewn with boulders, awaited them at a place Powell would name Disaster Falls. By the time they emerged, exhausted, men and supplies drenched, they had lost one boat, a third of their food, several weapons, and three barometers. George Bradley, the career soldier, wrote in his journal that evening, "It is a serious loss to us and we are rather low spirited tonight." Greater dangers and greater losses were ahead.

No one knew what lay around any bend of the river's coiling, rushing course. From Green River Station where they began, to the confluence of the Colorado and Virgin rivers where they would end, the route would descend a mile in elevation. Waterfalls, foaming rapids a mile or more in length, corkscrew whirlpools, and sheer cliffs a mile high would mark their descent deeper and deeper into the earth. Their boats capsized. Their oars were pulled from their hands. They flew over rocks or crashed into them. They portaged around some of the rapids, dragging the heavy boats to the point of exhaustion. Their food spoiled. The inescapable sun and blazing heat boiled and blinded them. Day after day after day, they confronted one impossible obstacle after another. Hungry, exhausted, barely escaping death again and again, they grappled with a despair that nearly incapacitated them at times. One man abandoned the project six weeks into the journey. Three others gave up only two days before its end. They scaled canyon cliffs to find an overland route home and were believed to have been murdered by Indians who mistook them for miners who had killed one of their women. By the end of June, a Salt Lake City newspaper reported the entire party save one had been drowned, the first of several reports of their demise.

The men didn't like the major much. They knew he had guts and admired him for it. But he was autocratic and remote, a scrawny, short man with a general's bearing and arrogance. They disliked the military discipline he imposed on them. And they doubted very much that he possessed the skill or knowledge to get them safely through his mad adventure. They suspected that even elemental common sense eluded him at times. A one-armed man who couldn't row, or help them portage, or haul himself back in the boat after he had been knocked overboard still thought he could scale the highest, sheerest, most daunting canyon walls by himself. He frequently left the expedition to take his measurements, collect his specimens, and make contact with local Indian tribes. He was nearly killed once falling from a rock face. One of the men rescued him by using his trousers as a rope to hoist him back up. On a later occasion, Powell had hung by his one arm from a ledge above a four-hundred-foot drop until his men rescued him again. The friction between Powell and his men was evident almost from the beginning and grew steadily worse throughout the journey. Most of the men regretted at one time or another their decision to follow him into the unknown. What renown and wealth they might have expected as rewards for their daring seemed little compensation for their suffering and hardly of consequence if no one of them would survive the trial.

All the while, marveling at the exotic and daunting landscape, studying its treasures, scaling the immense cliffs to measure them, giving names to the canyons, rapids, and natural monuments, scribbling his notes on brown pieces of paper, John Wesley Powell was finding answers to the vast catalog of questions that had tempted his irrational ambition to know the unknown and to risk all for the knowledge.

Powell marked the beginning of the Grand Canyon at the junction of the Colorado and Little Colorado (in fact, the canyon had begun sixty miles upriver). Camping there on the evening of August 12, eagerly anticipating the discoveries that were soon to be his, Powell wrote in his journal the words history has immortalized:

> We are now ready to start on our way down the Great Unknown. . . . We are three quarters of a mile in the depths of the earth, and the great river shrinks into insignificance, as it dashes its angry waves against the walls and cliffs that rise to the world above; they are but puny ripples, and we but pigmies, running up and down the sands, or lost among the boulders.
>
> We have an unknown distance yet to run; an unknown river yet to explore. What falls

there are, we know not; what rocks beset the channel, we know not; what walls rise over the river, we know not. Ah well, we may conjecture many things.

What he found was a land older than biblical time. And he was aware of the sublime implications of his discovery. Like Darwin, he must have experienced the surpassing fulfillment of glimpsing the true measure of history, extracted from the age-old geology of one of the most magnificent natural wonders on earth, and realizing that in that moment he possessed knowledge of time that quite possibly no other human being possessed.

"A library of the Gods," is how he described the canyon. The shelves "are not for books, but form the stony leaves of one great book.

He who would read the language of the universe may dig out letters here and there, and with them spell the words, and read, in a slow and imperfect way, but still so as to understand, the story of creation."

On August 30, ninety-eight days and a thousand miles since they had first launched the expedition, much sooner than they had anticipated, Powell and five of his men floated toward three men and a boy fishing at the mouth of the Virgin River. They were starved and worn out, but exhilarated, too. Powell, who would write a chronicle of the expedition that gained him international fame, might have been as tired and relieved as any of his crew, but he was wiser by a world than he had been when all he had were questions . . . and courage.

IT'S A GOOD THING to help your children become strong, to help build their fortitude. But more important are the lessons we teach them to kindle their desire for virtue in the hope that they will come to love it. Those lessons can begin almost immediately, before their feet reach the stirrups, their hands grasp the ball. Those, too, we impart by encouragement and experience, but the latter is more effective if it is the experience of observing us. We can exhort them to be honest. We can tell them the story of George Washington and the cherry tree. We can encourage them to read and take to heart the stories of good men and women, to enjoy and admire the tales of honest heroes. We can make observations about people they know or people who are in the news for some exceptional act of honesty, the person who finds a bag of cash and gives it to the police not a dollar short. Such instruction will start them thinking about honesty, their own measure of it and the occasions when it might be tested.

But if we want to really plant the seed of desire deep in their hearts, we should act virtuously. That means more than just striking a virtuous pose. "Now, Johnny, did you see what Daddy did? He told the nice cashier that she gave us too much change back." We should live as we wish them to live, honestly, justly, compassionately. Live it not ostentatiously but routinely, without remark. My father was the most honest man I've ever known. He wouldn't tell a lie, ever. He wouldn't shift the blame for his own mistake to a subordinate. He wouldn't seek to escape an uncomfortable situation by offering a contrived excuse or telling a comforting untruth. He would stand the consequences for his honesty, whatever they were. And he never remarked on it. I have not lived as honestly as he did. It's a struggle. But whenever I've been less than honest, I've felt ashamed and much worse than had I told the truth and taken the consequences. And I desire to do better because I loved him and his virtue. When I've shown any courage, it's more for the love of my father's virtue than his love of Admiral Nelson.

Our children love us. They love us and want to be sure of our love. So they desire to emulate us. They may first desire our virtue for the love of us. If we are true enough, they will come to love us for our virtue. They remember us when we're gone when they prove their own virtue, when they have learned to love virtue and fear the loss of it. That fear can prove stronger than the fear of embarrassment, or the fear of misfortune, or the fear of pain, or even the fear of existential threats. It's the fear that gives us courage.

Remorse, that most insistent of emotions, troubles us all from time to time. It's more acute and lasting than any discomfort caused by acting on a principle. I doubt many of us reach old age still nursing injuries inflicted on us long ago for following the demands of our conscience. They slip from memory easily, no matter how bitterly we experienced them at the time. I'm not one to take insult or injury lightly. On the contrary, I'm pretty quick to take offense. But I've always been surprised by just how soon I forget it. Yet I can recall all too well those times I've avoided the risk of injury or disappointment by overruling the demands of my conscience. I remember almost every one of them. Fearing a loss of virtue, for me, anyway, is more a fear of the inevitable remorse that follows. You can live with pain. You can live with disappointment. You can live with embarrassment. Remorse is an awful companion. And whatever the unwelcome consequences of courage, they are unlikely to be worse than the discovery that you are less a man than you pretend to be.

I speak from experience. My sermons on living virtuously have too often failed to inspire me in difficult circumstances to do what I know to be the right thing. Cowardice is often a secret affair. Usually no one knows of our failure. You may believe the opposite to be true. Our political culture has a sort of reverse reverence for the infamous examples of chicanery that we all like to point at to affirm our public codes of behavior. Every politician whose reputation and life are ruined by his own dishonesty occasions yet another round of sage head nodding and mutual reassurance that "the cover-up is always worse than the crime." But in truth, people lie because, more often than not, it works. More often than not, lying doesn't attract unwanted public attention, it lets us escape it. For every public figure caught in a lie, many more have avoided public disgrace by lying.

Think of how much more true this is of people who aren't public figures, who don't have to reckon with reporters and political opponents scavenging their lives and records for some evidence of duplicity. We lie to get by. We lie to stay out of trouble or disentangle ourselves from uncomfortable situations. We lie to avoid giving or receiving offense. Granted, most of our lies are of the harmless, white variety. They don't trouble our conscience all that much, if at all. That's a big part of their attraction. They're practically unavoidable. But how many of us can claim that we never once told a serious lie, for purposes less benign than sparing ourselves or someone else a little discomfort? Those aren't so easy to forget, are they?

An active conscience has a long memory. It doesn't matter that others don't know. We know. And the knowledge leaves a worse wound than those inflicted on us by others. We feel our dignity degraded by our own action. That's why my father found it easier—safer, really—never to lie. Obviously this caused him some difficulty from time to time, but nothing like the difficulty he feared should he violate his code of honor.

There have been times when I've confessed to dishonesty hoping that self-incrimination would repair the wound. I hoped that by inviting criticism for my failure, I could restore not just my public image but my self-image; that I could reclaim my virtue, reaffirm my courage, and recover my dignity. But remorse isn't something you can send on its way with a curt "You were right." It waits for the next moment when your honesty or compassion or loyalty is tested. Then, if you succeed, remorse might quit its nagging for the time being.

By encouragement and example, expose your children to the concept of honor. Honor that's concerned not just with the preservation of one's own dignity, although that's an important part, but with the whole sense of it, the full character of honor. A sense of honor encompasses all the virtues, justice, loyalty, honesty, compassion, courage. It is concerned with more than one's own situation, one's own rights. It's concerned with the rights of others. But in the beginning, let them be proud. Let them care for their personal dignity. It is the first step in building their respect for the dignity of others and their empathy for those whose dignity is assailed. Don't encourage them to ignore injuries, but don't encourage them to fear them, either. You don't have to urge them to fight every bully who tries to humiliate them. Acknowledge the fact of it, the wrong of it, and explain that it takes courage to keep your dignity. And that dignity can't be taken from you, no matter how strong the opponent; it can only be surrendered. No humiliation will rob your self-respect, even if you are not able or willing to respond in kind. Your virtue, your sense of honor, gives you that.

In stories about heroes, they always keep their dignity. Some stories celebrate the humble martyr, the hero who has the courage to take it, the courage to endure suffering and misfortune. Without the strength to vanquish their enemy, they suffer but hold on to the object of their oppressor's cruelty: their dignity. "This is courage in a man," wrote Euripedes. "To bear unflinchingly what heaven sends."

Then there are the stories about

heroes who protect their dignity by striking back. They were my favorites growing up.

"It is better to die on your feet than to live on your knees!" declared Emiliano Zapata, a man with a sense of honor; a man with considerable courage who served many people beyond himself; a man with an iron hold on his own dignity and a genuine compassion for the dignity of his people. He couldn't stop fighting. He fought until his enemies killed him.

Few heroes loom as large in the traditions of the Navajo as Manuelito and Barboncito. The first, bellicose and impetuous, preferred to kill his enemies than treat with them; the second, a more peaceable sort, favored patience and reconciliation over armed struggle. But they fought together when they believed their dignity and that of their people could not be secured by other means.

As a boy, Manuelito was mocked by his friends for the pride and elegance of his bearing. "You walk like a chief," they teased, "and you haven't fought any battles."

"I walk like a chief now," he responded, "so that when I become one, I will already know how to behave."

When Navajo lands were still within the territory of Mexico, sixteen-year-old Manuelito accompanied a tribal leader to a peace conference with a delegation of Mexican officials at Santa Fe. The town's curious inhabitants gathered around the visiting delegation, staring spellbound at their proud, exotic appearance. Manuelito, over six feet tall, strode through the crowd, his broad shoulders back, his head

Chief Manuelito

BETTMANN/CORBIS

erect and staring straight ahead, his face fixed in solemnity, careful to avoid turning his gaze either right or left or down to meet the stares of the nervous gawkers who scattered before him as he walked. He cut quite a figure and relished his effect on the crowd. His people had serious grievances against the officials who tolerated the capture and enslavement of Navajo by marauding bands of Mexicans and the seizure of Navajo lands by Mexican settlers, and Manuelito was not a man for peace.

He was for war, and he thought of more than dazzling his enemies with his appearance. He wanted to strike terror into their hearts with his martial prowess. In council with Navajo elders, he argued for war and proved himself in battle when they acquiesced, dressed imposingly in a battle helmet made from the skin of a mountain lion he had killed. He became a chief.

During the Mexican War, when the United States took control of the territory of New Mexico and Arizona, Manuelito joined the leaders of other Navajo clans in signing an 1846 peace treaty with the Americans, the first of seven treaties calling for peace between the United States and the Navajo nation.

The Navajo were not like other Indian nations Americans were used to fighting and defeating and forcing ever farther west or onto desolate reservations. They did not live from hunt to hunt, from raid to raid. They raised cattle and sheep. They grew crops. They were prosperous. Manuelito was a prosperous man. And it wasn't long before Americans' claims on Navajo grazing land, their failure to stop Mexican slave raids, turned Manuelito against the new, stronger foreign intruders. An 1849 conference between Colonel John Washington and Navajo leader Narbona, Manuelito's father-in-law, who preferred diplomacy to fighting and had long tried to discourage his son-in-law's belligerent nature, had ended in a riot after a Mexican guide accompanying the American delegation accused the Navajo of stealing his horse. The ensuing violence ended when U.S. soldiers shot and killed seven Navajo, including Narbona. Manuelito's distrust of the Americans blazed into implacable enmity.

The establishment of the first American fort in Arizona, Fort Defiance, inaugurated a period of frequent skirmishing between Navajo and Americans over grazing, water, and livestock disputes. After soldiers burned Manuelito's village and crops, the "Angry Warrior" was determined to unite the Navajo clans in a war to drive the Americans from their land. First he had to convince Barboncito, one of the most influential of the Navajo chiefs, to fight.

Like Narbona, Barboncito, known to the Navajo as the Orator, had sought accommodation with the Americans. He had kept his tribe from joining the punitive livestock raiding and fighting that Manuelito and other clan leaders used to prosecute their grievances against the Americans. For nearly a decade, he had tried to mediate the disputes, and his had been the strongest Navajo voice against war. He was older, wiser, and he had been an influential leader long before Manuelito began to inspire the Navajo clans with his militant defiance. He had long been a staunch opponent of American encroachment of Navajo lands but had used his persuasiveness in negotiations to redress his grievances rather than resort to war with an enemy he knew was too powerful to be permanently defeated. But the destruction of Navajo villages, crops, and livestock had proved too grievous an injury to settle by negotiation, and he agreed to join Manuelito and a thousand Navajo warriors in an attack on Fort Defiance in 1860.

They nearly succeeded, but were eventually driven back by the soldiers' guns into the steep hideouts of the Chuska Mountains. From there they fought the Americans in a yearlong stalemate, until the fort was abandoned and the soldiers transferred to service in the Civil War.

A year later the soldiers came

back, now under the command of General James Carleton, an arrogant and self-regarding man with orders to subdue the Indian population of the Southwest, ambitious to prove himself to Washington and secure a more prestigious command in the Civil War. After first subjugating the Mescalero Apache, he appointed Colonel Kit Carson, famous scout, Indian trader, and Union soldier, to lead a column of soldiers and Ute mercenaries to force the Navajo from their lands and onto a reservation in the desert flats of the Pecos River valley in southeastern New Mexico, the Bosque Redondo. Carleton intended, he told Carson, to transform the Navajo from "heathens and raiders" into "settled Christians."

Mindful of the army's success against the Apache, Barboncito let

Carson know he was prepared to treat for peace, but not to move his people from their land. General Carleton would have none of it and issued a deadline for the Navajo to submit to relocation. "I will not go to the Bosque," Barboncito replied. "I will never leave my country, not even if it means I am killed." In the majestic red rock maze of the Canyon de Chelly, the sacred and once impregnable Navajo sanctuary, Barboncito and Manuelito prepared for war.

Carson knew better than to try to track the Navajo, a few war parties at a time, through the difficult and mysterious terrain. He initiated instead a scorched-earth campaign all across Navajo lands, burning villages, orchards, cornfields, and hogans, confiscating and killing livestock, leaving behind wherever he had marched his column a wasted landscape and a devastated people. Six months later, with the spirit of Navajo resistance nearly exhausted, Carson took the stronghold, its defenders reduced to hiding in caves and throwing rocks at the invaders, and forced eight thousand of the starving inhabitants on a three-hundred-mile march, the Long Walk, to the Bosque Redondo. Two hundred of their number perished on the march. Two thousand more would die from hunger and disease on their new reservation, with its scarce and foul water, drought-devastated soil, inadequate government supplies, and violent quarrels with the Apache with whom they were forced to share the land.

Barboncito had led his tribe to the reservation but refused to remain himself, and with five hundred warriors, he rode back to his country. He now intended not to fight the soldiers but to evade them and live free in his own country. Manuelito had refused to surrender. Surviving on hidden caches of corn, enduring Kit Carson's continued war of attrition against them and constant attacks by the soldiers' Ute and Mexican allies, the two chiefs led an ever dwindling band of warriors that ranged beyond the western extremes of their lands in an extraordinarily courageous campaign of defiance. When Carleton sent Navajo leaders from the reservation to plead with Manuelito to surrender for their sake, he refused. "Tell Carleton I have nothing to lose but my life, and they can come and take that whenever they please." But by September 1866, with only twenty-three starving followers still at his command, Manuelito surrendered and made the long walk to the Bosque Redondo. Barboncito held out for another two months before he too submitted to the authority of the United States and came down from the high cliff walls of the Canyon de Chelly. Once he arrived at the reservation, however, he couldn't bear the desolate remove from Navajo country. He escaped and returned to the canyon again, but he was soon recaptured and forced to share the unhappy reservation life of his people.

General Carleton was relieved of his command two years later, not as a reward for his subjugation of the Navajo, but in reproach by his superiors, who were exasperated by his cruel methods. Manuelito and other clan leaders, dispirited and weakened by their bleak captivity, appealed to Barboncito to plead with the white authorities to let the Navajo return in peace to their country. Barboncito's courage had never ebbed. For two years on the reservation, by exhortation and in sacred ceremonies, he had encouraged the Navajo to believe that they would eventually be freed and allowed to go home. Now he would speak for all the Navajo in a council with General William Tecumseh Sherman. As Maunelito and the other leaders watched, Barboncito retrieved an unused pair of moccasins and put them on. "These are my last pair," he told them. "I've saved them for many months. These I will wear out walking home with you."

Sherman told the leaders that he recognized the reservation could not sustain their people and urged them to agree to another relocation to the east, to a reservation in Oklahoma, a place where the Cherokee had lived in peace and comparative prosperity for many years. No, Barboncito replied, they could not go to Oklahoma. "I hope to God you will not ask us to go to another country. . . . It will be another Bosque Redondo."

He explained that since the Navajo "were first created, four mountains and four rivers were pointed out to us by the First Woman of the Navajo. It was told to us by our forefathers that we were never to move east of the Rio Grande or west of the San Juan River and I think our coming here has been the cause of so much death among us and our animals."

Sherman made the case for the civilized life they could learn to live in Oklahoma, under the paternal care of the government. "It will be cheaper there than here. We will give you schools in English or Spanish." He urged the Navajo to "send some of your wisest men" there to "see for themselves."

"If we are taken back to our own country," Barboncito promised, "we will call you our father and mother. . . . I am speaking for the whole tribe. It appears to me that the General commands the whole thing as a god. . . . I am speaking to you now as if I were speaking to a spirit, and I wish you to tell me when you are going to take us to our own country."

Moved by the speaker's eloquence and determination, and impressed by his assurances to respect the government's authority and abide by the terms of their consent, Sherman and the other commissioners agreed to return the Navajo to their country, not all of it, but a smaller holding guaranteed by treaty to the Navajo forever. In exchange, Barboncito agreed to become head chief of the whole nation. He assumed responsibility for ensuring that the terms of the new treaty, which restricted their cultivation and grazing to within the boundaries of the reservation, and forbade the restless young Navajo men to raid or retaliate against their neighbors, not be violated.

Barboncito, Manuelito, and more than seven thousand Navajo returned to their country in the summer of 1868. An old man now, Barboncito accepted his responsibility, though he did not want it. He struggled to keep the young men in line. He rode out himself to patrol the trails from which they raided, returned stolen livestock, and impressed the leaders of Mormon settlers with his sense of honor. Three years after he returned to his country, following a long ride in cold weather to discourage some young warriors from raiding, he became mortally ill. He died in the Canyon de Chelly, where he had been born and where his people still live to this day.

One man had been strong and proud, a firebrand, who proved he had the courage to fight almost as hard and as long as his pride demanded. But neither his courage nor his strength, though very great, was inexhaustible. The other, wiser man also had exemplary courage and pride. He too could fight longer than others. But he had the courage to endure defeat without despair, without losing hope. His courage proved the stronger and more effective of the two.

THE DEFENSIVE KIND of courage, the capacity to suffer with dignity, without losing hope, is a virtue that can be possessed by the physically strong and weak alike, though it is perhaps even harder to possess than the courage to take offensive action to right a wrong or discharge a duty. It is the courage of the conscientious, whether it finds expression on the battlefield or abhors violent action. It can be possessed by pacifists who believe that violence, no matter the justice of its object, is always immoral. It must be voluntary, however, to be courage.

Enduring an inescapable fate stoically is admirable, but it is not the same thing as courage. Suffering stoically a terrible fate that you could have escaped, but that your convictions, your sense of honor, compelled you to accept, is. The Christians sacrificed to the lions chose not to be sacrificed, but to be Christians. The politics and bigotry of the Romans consigned them to a violent end, which they could have avoided by renouncing their faith. But they didn't choose death. They chose to keep their faith, their hope of eternal life, and suffer the consequences. Whether they suffered them stoically or were dragged to the experience pleading for their lives is beside the point. Keeping their faith required courage superior to the resolve of a person who accepts unwanted but unavoidable trouble with admirable composure. The object of courage isn't just a handsome comportment or a physical expression of strength.

Courage must be conscientious of duty if it is to claim the distinction of being the first, indispensable virtue. It is much more than mental toughness or "grace under pressure," as Hemingway defined it. For years I thought it was. And when asked for a definition of courage, I usually quoted Hemingway's response. But I learned that people who cry out in despair, who are seized by mortal terror, can still act heroically. Although courageous people often appear to act gracefully under pressure, and their dignified, disciplined behavior produces some of the most lasting images in fiction and history, it isn't grace that proclaims their courage, but their decision to face the pressure at all, and face it for reasons greater than simply to prove to themselves or others that they could do it with aplomb.

Face the experience with quiet

assurance or with a look that reflects stark terror, screaming in anguish all the while. It doesn't really matter. What matters is that you faced it, lived it, and did so because your conscience compelled you to act. That is what gives courage its grandeur. Even Christ on the cross, my faith's most exalted example of courage, cried out in desperation, "Father, Father, why have You forsaken me?" It is not Christ's reticence in a moment of agony that we worship. It is because he accepted his duty to love, a love incarnate—God become man to redeem humanity by love—and the awful suffering his duty demanded that we exalt the singular courage of his sacrifice.

Too great a distinction is made between moral courage and physical courage. They are in many instances the same. For either to be authentic,

it must encounter fear and prove itself superior to that fear. I mean fear
that is a rational response to a real
threat, something more rational
than a phobia. No doubt it is difficult to overcome a fear of public
speaking, but I think we deprive
courage of its exceptional quality
when we ascribe it to those who
do overcome such things, admirable though the accomplishment is.
Therapy isn't courage. I distinguish
courage from fortitude and discipline. Both are qualities common in
courageous people, admirable qualities, but they're not courageous in
themselves. By fear I mean fear of
serious harm to our well-being,
physical or otherwise, that wars
with our need to take action but is
overcome because we value something or someone more than our
own well-being. In our blessed and
progressive society there may be

fewer occasions when we need be afraid to be virtuous, when we need our courage to remain so, but still they are more numerous than the occasions when we need more than our conscience, when we need physical strength and skill, to act.

A sense of honor and duty, a regard for the dignity of others, and the shame we feel when we neglect them motivate both physical and moral courage. More often than not, they are almost exactly the same. The greatest acts of moral courage are usually those that confront a physical danger without the means or intent to offer such physical danger in return. Sometimes we can see distinctions between the truest moral and physical courage. The means employed by each are sometimes distinct, as is the nature of the occasion when each is summoned. Physical courage is more often employed to defend or obtain a tangible, physical object or condition. Moral courage is concerned with the defense of a moral principle. Thus, I think it can be fairly said that physical courage can be, and has been, possessed for bad ends, by bad people. Hitler was a brave soldier in World War I. The world would have been a lot better off had he been as physically craven as he was morally destitute. Moral courage is defined by the virtues that are its object.

We sometimes recognize another distinction between moral and physical courage in the nature of the threat they must face. Physical courage is often needed to overcome our fear of the consequences of failure, the soldier who thinks, If I don't take out that enemy machine gun, my buddies and I are going to die here. Moral courage, more often than not, confronts the fear of the consequences of our success, the corporate whistle-blower who thinks, If I expose this wrong, its perpetrators will demote or fire me, or the person who objects to abuse inflicted unjustly on another, knowing that the bully might turn his attention to him in retribution.

The distinction isn't present in every instance of physical and moral courage, but it is often the case. And it is more accurate than the idea that holds two kinds of courage distinct because one faces a physical threat and the other doesn't. Both quite often do. Are both moral and physical courage possessed by people who risk imprisonment to defend their rights and those of others, even though they won't be tortured in captivity? It's hard to tell the difference, isn't it? Both seem to obtain in such circumstances. In many instances, the exercise of moral courage only results in some form of social alienation or embarrassment or psychological distress. It may still be courage that confronts the nonphysical threat, but it should be distinguished in degree from the courage that confronts violent opposition, even though both are concerned not just with our self-interest, but with the dignity of others.

"If a man hasn't discovered something that he will die for, he isn't fit to live." Martin Luther King Jr. made that observation in 1963. Leaving aside that the obsessively greedy, the power mad, and the psychopath might prefer to die than live without the objects they desire, we still take his point. Better to suffer for a good cause than live safely without one. Dr. King's cause was the dignity of his race and the full realization of America's founding values. He is, rightly, held up as an exemplar of moral courage. He was a believer in nonviolence who had courage of conscience, the courage to resist repression, to live his moral code. But we cannot differentiate his courage from physical courage. He suffered violence done to his well-being. He was murdered for his willingness to act on his beliefs, a fate many of his admirers believe he anticipated and must have feared. Yet fear did not restrain him. It thus seems fair to observe that Martin Luther King Jr. had the physical courage to defend his moral convictions without resorting to violence. He had the courage to face the possible, if not probable, consequences of his success. How different is that kind of courage from the soldier's?

In some instances, it may be more sublime than the soldier's because of the asymmetry of the act of courage and its opposing force, and the increase in the probability of suffering it entails for the person who has the courage to face an enemy unarmed, as it were. If it takes courage to kill or be killed in war, it is a courage often prompted by an instinct for survival. And your courage is responding to the threat in, if not exactly equal measures, at least measures that are not essentially opposite. The soldier, no matter how daunting the odds, usually acts with the hope that he has a fighting chance. But the person who forswears violence while intent on challenging a violent threat must have hope of something greater than survival.

During my congressional career, I've had the privilege to become acquainted and friendly with John Lewis, one of Dr. King's bravest disciples. On a Sunday in March 1965, John Lewis was as courageous as anyone could ever hope to be. His was not a spontaneous courage that appeared inexplicably, almost mysteriously, in a fearsome moment. He had practiced courage for much of his young life. He had chosen a life that required him constantly to summon it from a deep well inside of him that he kept replenished by faith and suffering. He had courage that wouldn't quit, the rarest kind.

He was born in the thoroughly segregated Alabama of 1940 into a stable, virtuous family, the third of his hardworking, sharecropper parents' ten children, raised in a house without running water or electricity, expected to work alongside his siblings until sunset every day but Sunday in the backbreaking toil of the cotton fields. Sunday was the Lord's day, and the Lewis family hitched their mule to the wagon and traveled several miles to their Baptist church for a day of service and fellowship with their co-religionists. He recalls seeing only two white men in the early years of his childhood: the mailman and a traveling salesman.

A religious boy, moved by the Holy Spirit to preach, he tended the family chickens with the dedication of a minister tending his congregation. He preached to them, baptized them, gave the eulogy at their funerals, and tried vainly to defend them from the ax. He was a teenager when he heard a radio broadcast of a Martin Luther King Jr. sermon and found his calling.

He attended the American Baptist Theological Seminary in Nashville and studied for the ministry. There he met and became a disciple of a Vanderbilt professor,

John Lewis, spattered with blood after being attacked and beaten by pro-segregationists in Montgomery, Alabama, during the Freedom Rides, May 20, 1961.

James Lawson, who taught the Gandhian discipline of nonviolent civil disobedience, a radical pacifism then most notably espoused by Dr. King, which required its adherents to oppose injustice by breaking unjust laws and taking whatever punishment came, peacefully. He became a leader in a student-led campaign to integrate Nashville lunch counters, suffering verbal and physical abuse from decidedly non-Gandhian sons and daughters of the old Confederacy and resulting in his frequent arrest by white authorities. In 1961, he and his friends joined the famous Freedom Riders, who were attempting to integrate bus lines across the South. He was attacked and beaten by a bunch of white thugs in the waiting room of a bus terminal in Rock Hill, South Carolina. He was knocked unconscious in Montgomery, Alabama, when some redneck swung a wooden soda crate at his head.

Gandhian discipline proved a heavy burden against such tactics, and, fearing even worse violence, some civil rights leaders advocated pulling out of the campaign. Lewis kept at it. With the head wound he suffered in Montgomery wrapped in a cloth bandage, he was arrested in Jackson, Mississippi, and sentenced to thirty days at Parchman Prison Farm, where the guards carried cattle prods and tried to beat the nonviolence out of him. Soon after, the Interstate Commerce Commission ordered southern bus lines to integrate.

"I was caught up in the spirit of history," Lewis recalled. And the spirit moved him inexorably toward even greater danger.

He and his compatriots had led the integration of Nashville, and

John was elected chairman of the Student Nonviolent Coordinating Committee (SNCC). He won admirers among the senior leadership of the civil rights movement, in the Congress for Racial Equality (CORE) and the Southern Christian Leadership Conference (SCLC), including Dr. King. He marched with them on Washington in 1963 and gave a fiery speech, critical of the Kennedy administration, at the Lincoln Memorial.

In the summer of 1966, the SNCC and CORE recruited white students from northern states to help southern blacks register to vote. They chose to focus their campaign in Mississippi, a bastion of segregation, where southern bigotry was as obdurately defiant as had been the Confederate defenders at Vicksburg in the Civil War. The ferocity of their violent opposition to the full emancipation of black southerners was enough to cause many activists to doubt the continued efficacy of nonviolent civil disobedience. Three white kids from the North were kidnapped and murdered by Ku Klux Klan terrorists. No one, no matter his idealism or courage, could have willed away the tight grip of fear that must have clutched the stoutest hearts in Mississippi that summer. Some got so scared that they left. Others got angry, losing their faith in the ethic of nonviolence. Some competed for the hearts and minds of disenfranchised blacks, their voices starting to drown out appeals to persevere in peaceful dignity to change the hearts of their adversaries by shaming them, arguing it was easier to change hearts by scaring the hell out of them. Even the goal of integration was cast aside by some, and in its place the surer appeal of an easier pride, black separatism, rose to claim popular support.

John Lewis was one of the bravest of those who stayed true to the faith. They couldn't scare the courage out of him. They couldn't beat it out of him, either. By the time he got to Selma, Alabama, they had teargassed him, arrested him, and beaten him more times than he could remember. They had scared him all they could.

In the first weeks of 1965, he led a group of mostly elderly blacks to the steps of the courthouse in Selma, Alabama. As he recalled years later, Sheriff "Jim Clarke was waiting, gun on one hip, nightstick on the other, and an electric cattle prod in his hand." The cattle prod, a weapon used on animals, symbolized the rejection of black humanity that the tradition of southern bigotry insisted upon. Addressing him by name, Clarke showed what he meant. "John Lewis, you're an outside agitator. You are the lowest form of humanity."

"I may be an agitator," Lewis responded, "but I'm no outsider. I was born ninety miles from here. And we're going to stay here until these people can register."

They stayed for a week. Three thousand people were arrested. Many more were abused, terrorized by threats and violence. Writing in *The Washington Post,* Lewis remembered, "A young man named Jimmy Lee was shot in the stomach when he stepped in to protect his grandfather. He died from his wounds several days later. The plan to march from Selma to Montgomery was our response."

There was resentment within the SNCC, which had been trying to register blacks for years, when Martin Luther King Jr. and the other SCLC leaders got involved late in 1964, bringing the national press with them. And when the SCLC announced the march to Montgomery after the killing at Selma's courthouse, many of Lewis's associates were annoyed by the presumption of leadership. The day before the march was to begin, Governor George Wallace announced that their protest would not be permitted, and Jim Clarke began deputizing every local white man over twenty-one. Most of the SNCC leaders thought it wise to withdraw from the march. Lewis went to Atlanta to argue for their participation. They would agree to let him and a few others march only as individuals, not as SNCC representatives.

King had been detained in Montgomery, so Lewis and Hosea

Williams of the SCLC led the march. In the afternoon of March 7, 1965, remembered forever after as "Bloody Sunday," the demonstrators, a majority of them women and most of them old folks, met at Brown Chapel AME Church, where Lewis gave them their final instructions. The marchers were to remain orderly no matter what happened. They were not to defend themselves with weapons or carry anything that could be mistaken for a weapon. They shouldn't sing, chant, or even talk.

Lewis and Williams marched at the head of the column, more than five hundred strong, toward the Edmund Pettus Bridge spanning the Alabama River. He was dressed in a suit and tie, as were most of the marchers, and wore a tan raincoat against the cool breeze that blew that day. They were supposed to be headed for Montgomery, but none of them expected to reach there. They didn't know how far they would get, but they knew something would happen long before they made the fifty miles to Montgomery. They walked a mile, hardly uttering a sound, past lines of white hecklers waving the Confederate flag, before they reached the bridge.

When they reached the crest of the bridge, all were silent, a strange, unnatural silence. Strange, as silence is always strange in an atmosphere that is pregnant with impending change. No calm had settled over Selma to urge the quiet. Everything was alive with apprehension, with expectation. Something momentous and terrible was coiled, waiting for the marchers to walk close enough to strike.

In his wise and compassionate memoir of the civil rights movement, Lewis recalled the sight the marchers beheld on the Edmund Pettus Bridge and the noise that shattered the silence that afternoon. "There, facing us at the bottom of the other side, stood a sea of white-helmeted, blue-uniformed Alabama State Troopers, line after line of them." Hundreds of troopers and sheriff's deputies, many on horse-back, were carrying clubs and prods and whips and wearing gas masks. The troopers' commander ordered the marchers to disperse: "You have two minutes to turn around and go back." Lewis suggested they kneel where they were and pray. As they did, the force opposing them advanced. "I remember how vivid the sounds were," Lewis wrote, "as the troopers rushed us—the clunk of the troopers' heavy boots, the whoops of rebel yells from the white onlookers, the clip-clop of horses' hooves hitting the hard asphalt of the highway, the voice of a woman shouting, 'Get 'em! Get the niggers!' "

That evening, ABC News interrupted its normal programming to broadcast a tape of the terrible violence that ensued. Millions of Americans saw the marchers—peaceful, dignified, well dressed, kneeling in humble resistance—scattered and overrun by what appeared to be enraged authorities, striking them with clubs and whips, chasing them as they fled, trampling them beneath horse hooves. They heard Sheriff Clarke yell, "Get the goddamn niggers!" They saw old men and women fall. They saw the blood stream from their heads and soak into their clothes. And they saw John Lewis take the first blow, a baton thrust to his stomach, shoving him back on the marchers behind him. And then the second, a hard-swung club to the left side of his head, blood pouring from the wound, darkening his raincoat, leaving a permanent inch-long scar where it had struck. They saw Lewis, lying on the ground, valiantly lift his head and try to struggle to his feet. They saw him collapse unconscious from the effort, his skull fractured, his brain concussed.

They saw dignified people, claiming their constitutional right to a government derived from their consent, disobey the law that denied them that right—without anger, without malice, without the least threat of violence. The saw men and women affirming the promise of the Declaration of Independence, with its premise of a universal right to liberty, whipped and clubbed for their patriotism. And they were ashamed of their country. They were ashamed of themselves, ashamed that they had not loved their country as much as the marchers; that they had not the courage to march into the force of such injustice.

They were still watching ten days later when President Johnson gave his famous "We shall overcome" address before the Congress, announcing the introduction of the Voting Rights Act. "At times history and fate meet at a single time in a single place to shape a turning point in man's unending search for freedom," Johnson said. "So it was at Lexington and Concord. So it was a century ago at Appomattox. So it was last week at Selma."

John Lewis wrote, "When I care about something, I'm prepared to take the long, hard road . . . that's what faith is all about." His faith is

his country and the justice it prom-
ises. Like Dr. King, he believes it is
possible in this country to create
the "beloved community," where
all races, all religious persuasions, all
hearts, live together peacefully, re-
spectfully, where people can "lay
down the burden of race . . . just lay
it down."

The rise of black nationalism and
its abandonment of the discipline
of nonviolence, fired all the more
by the violence at Selma, claimed
more adherents. The SNCC replaced John Lewis as chairman
with Stokely Carmichael. American
cities burned. Racial resentments
hardened. Dr. King was murdered.

Lewis lost his bearings for a time
in New York City, a shy country
boy amid the noise, distractions, and
pleasures of the city. Recovering
his purpose, he served in the Carter
administration and on Atlanta's city

council. And in 1986, he was elected to Congress from Georgia's fifth district, where he serves today.

He still speaks out in opposition to those who envision an America divided by race. He denounced Reverend Louis Farrakhan and the hate and anti-Semitism he shared with his lieutenant, Khalid Muhammad, calling them, rightly, "bigots." He took considerable heat for that pronouncement. But he stood by it. And he stands by his Gandhian discipline, the dignified humility of courageous nonviolence. "The means by which we struggle must be consistent with the ends we seek," he explains.

I've seen courage in action on many occasions. I can't say I've seen anyone possess more of it, and use it for any better purpose and to any greater effect, than John Lewis.

He recalled thinking in the moments before he lost consciousness on the Edmund Pettus Bridge, People are going to die here. I'm going to die here. But like Roy Benavidez, Lewis could make the rarest of claims, that "there is a certain point where you move beyond fear, and I had reached that point.

"You lose your sense of fear. Because as long as you're afraid, the opposition has something over you."

The force of his character, his sense of honor, built from hard work, honesty, dutifulness, and loving encouragement on an Alabama sharecropper's farm, from the inspiration of his heroes and the principles they imparted to him, kept up his courage on the "long, hard road." And his courage has kept his faith, a faith he has had many occasions to doubt—the faith in the possibility of the beloved community, "not hateful, not violent, not uncaring . . . not separated, not polarized, not adversarial." And probably not attainable in this life, sinners that we all are. But certainly worth the struggle, worth the sacrifice, worth the courage.

IT TAKES COURAGE to defend your own dignity; sometimes it requires extraordinary heroism. Yet often its wellspring is anger and wounded pride, a source we can't always rely upon to incite us to action. I am familiar with that kind of courage, and it took me many years to recognize its limitations. It can be used up more quickly than you might have imagined when your sense of honor is self-absorbed, inert, not galvanized by empathy for the experiences of others.

A mature sense of honor encompasses more than the respect for our rights that we insist on from others. Our sense of honor must cross the divide between vanity and righteousness by insisting on the universality of our principles. It is not enough to be honest and just and demand that we be treated honestly and justly by others. We must learn to love honesty and justice for themselves, not just for their effect on our personal circumstances, but for their effect on the world, on the whole of human experience, on the progress of humanity in which we have played our part. People I have known or known of who possessed a mature sense of honor seem to have not lost their self-regard, but sublimated it to a regard for themselves as part of that enterprise. They see existential threats in assaults on the dignity of others.

They are uncommon people. It takes great courage to defend the dignity of others. But it is a courage that may not be so easily depleted, paradoxically, even though the demands on it are more numerous. Perhaps that's because while they share the experience of suffering, they share the burden of courage in response to it.

In prison, I was not always a match for my enemies. I was proud and angry. I thought I was tough, clever, and prepared enough to resist. But I found my courage wanting nevertheless. When it failed it was because my primary concern had been my own survival, my own dignity. I relied on my own resources to guard them, and my courage ran out much earlier than I had expected.

Fortunately, I shared my circumstances with hundreds of brave men who insisted on a communal code of conduct—we would all return with honor. Each man's suffering was our shared concern, each man's resistance our shared responsibility.

We didn't relieve one another of the demands of honor. Each man was expected to resist to the best of his ability. But we relied on one another to strengthen our ability, to encourage us when we felt used up, to assure us that there was no dishonor in trying but falling short of how we perceived our duty in one instance, if we recovered and tried again. And we honored a chain of command that supplemented our own understanding of our duty, of its demands and its limits, so that we would not think ourselves cowards for having an exhaustible supply of courage. When we saw both our duty and our courage as a common experience, our duty was easier to bear and our courage more at the ready. We completed one another's sense of honor, and it made us stronger. Remarkably, no more than a mere handful of us returned without our honor, having lost the courage it demanded. Had each of us been kept in separate prisons, unable to communicate with one another, to share one another's experiences, to depend on one another, had we been forced to rely on our individual pride and strength, many more of us would have lost our courage and our honor.

We do not begin life fearing losses suffered by others. We are born selfish and struggle against it all our lives. We are concerned with our self-regard, although we might recognize it is dependent on the approval of our family. Later, the circle of those whose good opinion we require widens to encompass our friends. When does the moment occur when concern for our own dignity enlarges to encompass the dignity of others? I think the transformation must begin when our desire to be loved becomes love for the object of our desire. And it progresses when our desire to emulate the behavior of our beloved, to ensure their love, becomes a love for the virtues that constitute their character. In that moment our conscience is born, our capacity to see that what's right for us is right for others. "If a man be brave," wrote the Unitarian social reformer James Freeman Clarke, "let him obey his conscience."

Clarke had borrowed from Goethe his life's motto: "Do your nearest duty." It's not always as easy as it sounds, to see your nearest duty or to want to see it. It's even harder to anticipate when our children will recognize their nearest duty. It's as hard for us to recognize sometimes as it is for them. We may not want to recognize it because we fear for them more than they fear for themselves, and their nearest duty might contain risks to their immediate happiness or worse. We can pay attention to them as they recount their day at school or on the playground, and identify in the routine occurrences of their experience an occasion where a duty would have appeared to a good person, with the choice to risk something or not to do it. But we don't always want to, even if we know that what they risk isn't something of lasting value.

We want our children to be popular almost as much as our children want to be popular. Popularity offers temporary security, enhances confidence, eases the petty disappointments of youth, and can be confused for love. But it's not love. It has no moral quality. It's a condition that might be hard to attain for some but doesn't represent an achievement of lasting significance. Its effects aren't as determinative of the quality of life as you might think when you're young and crave it. But still our children want to be popular, and we want them to be. If they are not, if they have suffered some embarrassment, some reduction in their circumstances in the constant ups and downs of childhood society, we'll try to comfort and encourage them by observing how transitory and ultimately insignificant a thing is popularity. But they'll feel the loss of it just the same, as will we. We hurt for them, and while we might know the hurt will pass, we would not want them to risk it again unnecessarily.

Teaching them virtue in the abstract, without recommending it in a specific situation, is not such a demanding thing. We don't experience empathetic apprehension and pain by urging them to be always honest, always fair, always respectful, the virtues that will alert them of their duty. We don't usually imagine their possession of those virtues provoking much more than the admiration of adults, their teachers, our neighbors and friends. If we're honest, we have in the backs of our minds as we impart these lessons to our children our own pride, our regard for our children as a reflection of our parenting. We want them to be honest and respectful because they and we will be admired for it. It's the allure of popularity that afflicts adults no less than children.

So it can be quite hard to help our children recognize their nearest duty if by so doing they risk social embarrassment or alienation from the peers whose friendship they most desire. But for kids, those are the most common risks of doing your nearest duty. In fact, they are the most common risks we adults face in our settled, mostly tranquil country.

What do you do when, in the course of your children's recitation of the day's events, they mention how bad they felt when their friend, the most popular girl or boy in their crowd, was cruel to a child with few friends, made the child cry from embarrassment and loneliness? We tell them that it's right to feel bad about it, as we should about any cruelty inflicted on the innocent. But don't we hesitate to tell them what they should do beyond empathizing with the victim? Maybe we recommend that they seek out the child and offer their companionship, even though we recognize such an act of decency might risk some opprobrium from the person who caused the injury. But do we recommend our children confront that popular boy or girl whose friendship they enjoy and tell them they think less of them for their unkindness? We might, but usually not without hesitation, dreading the impact it might have on our children's happiness. It's hard to tell children to recognize their nearest duty and to make the choice to accept it, when we know they may suffer for it.

When the pangs of our conscience confront our dread of the consequences for our loved ones who answer the call of theirs, it's our own courage we must summon as much as theirs. We have to believe in the truths we utter to our children when they are the ones who have been hurt, treated unkindly for no reason. We have to believe that there really is no great significance to being popular. We have to believe that if we love and are loved, by our family, by our true friends, and from that love we become good, the loss of popularity will hurt no longer than a bee sting. People who have only popularity to recommend themselves to our memory are soon forgotten. People with virtue, who do their nearest duty as their conscience instructs, are remembered. They are remembered as a source of happiness, not someone who resents another's.

We cannot explain virtue just in the abstract to them and hope that somehow they'll be okay. We have to help them recognize virtue's opposite and to feel an outrage that incites us to action and to accept the consequences. Keep the consequences in perspective, know that they are not the worst things in life, but accept them; accept them and resolve to provoke them again when virtue demands.

Almost every Israeli child is taught to learn by heart a poem written by a young Jewish girl sixty years ago:

> *Blessed is the match consumed*
> *in kindling flame.*
> *Blessed is the flame that burns*
> *in the secret fastness of the*
> *heart.*
> *Blessed is the heart with*
> *strength to stop*
> *its beating for honor's sake.*
> *Blessed is the match consumed*
> *in kindling flame.*

According to her mother, when Hannah Senesh, a precocious, intelligent, and conscientious child, was sixteen years old, her classmates elected her to an office in her elite Budapest high school's literary soci-

Hannah Senesh

COURTESY OF THE
SENESH FAMILY

ety. Attending her first meeting of the society, Hannah was informed by its older members that being a Jew disqualified her from accepting the office. When a new election was held and one of her friends was elected to replace her, she suffered the injury stoically. When her friend refused the office, Hannah instructed her to "accept it calmly, and don't think for an instance that I begrudge it to you. Not at all. If you don't accept it, someone else will. After all, it has nothing to do with whether Hannah Senesh or Maria X is more capable of fulfilling the assignment, but whether the person is a Jew or a Gentile."

Henceforth she would refuse all appeals to participate in the society's activities, as she would later decline an offer of admission to a university because she had graduated the top of her class. Only Jews who had graduated with the highest honors were admitted, while far less qualified Christians were accepted. She had been wronged. But it caused no injury to her self-esteem. Hers was not so weak that it could be hurt by another's lack of honor. Hannah looked only to the strength of her character for security.

She was born into a Hungarian family privileged with wealth and celebrity. Her father had been a famous playwright, an upstanding, principled man who loved his children and saw to their comfort and their character, although a bad heart killed him when they were still very young. Her mother was also a writer and, judging from the tender eloquence of her memoir of Hannah, as equally devoted to them and as decent as their father.

Owing to the contemptible political culture of much of Europe in the 1920s and 1930s, their privilege was circumscribed by the prevalent anti-Semitism of the time. But they prospered, lived well, and felt secure for the most part, even as the calamity of Nazi barbarism was gathering destructive power.

Hannah began a diary when she was thirteen, which she kept most of her life, filling it with more than the daily joys and trials of a girl's life. Some of the thoughts confided there are genuinely profound, as are her poems. Diaries amplify the ego's voice, emphasizing the writer's sensitivity to injuries and successes. They are often the practice of a budding existentialist. There is some of that to be found in Hannah's memoir. "I've become a vegetarian," she proudly announces to herself. "I would rather be an unusual person than average." But much of her diary has a less egocentric voice. Its pages are suffused with deeply felt compassion and the reflections of a just person. She had the perspective of a writer who seems to appreciate from a very early age her place in humanity, with natural rights equal to all others, but equal obligations, too, with a sense of belonging to something greater than her own experience.

In one of the earliest entries, she records a visit to her father's grave:

> How sad that we had to become acquainted with the cemetery so early in life. But I feel that even from beyond the grave Daddy is helping us, if in no other way than with his name. I don't think he could have left us a greater legacy.

And later:

> I'm actually with him in thought every evening, asking whether he is satisfied with me, whether my behavior pleases him.

Hannah was seventeen when she confided to her diary that she had become a Zionist:

> One needs to feel that one's life has meaning, that one is needed in this world.

Soon after she embraced the cause of a Jewish homeland, she became determined to immigrate to Palestine. Her mother tried to dissuade her while Hannah tried to persuade her mother to accompany her. Her mother recalls her explaining that "even if she had not been born a Jew she would still be on the side of the Jews because one must help . . . a people who were being treated so unjustly."

She left as soon as she graduated from high school, intent on matriculating at the agriculture school at Nahalal. Her mother preferred, sensibly, that she go to a university, where her learning and intelligence would serve her better. Her daughter replied, "There are already far too many intellectuals in Palestine; the great need is for workers who can help build the country."

She went to Palestine and enrolled in the agriculture school, graduating two years later with honors. Following graduation, she visited several kibbutzim before she chose to join a new settlement temporarily quartered in Haifa, pending relocation to permanent quarters near the ruins of the ancient Roman city of Caesarea. She threw herself into her new life and country with characteristic enthusiasm. She learned to speak and write Hebrew. She wished to communicate in the language of Eretz Yisrael, the ancestral Jewish homeland that Hannah and her fellow settlers hoped would be returned someday to Jewish political control. She deliberately chose not to join a kibbutz established by other Hungarian immigrants, but preferred to plunge into her new life and to hasten the time when everything that was so strange to her now—the land, the customs, the people whose background, language, and society was so different from her upbringing—would be comfortably familiar.

But she was lonely, too. She missed and worried about her mother, still in Budapest, and her brother, who had been trapped in

France after the German invasion. She made few friends at Nahalal and none at Caesarea. Her diary entries during her four years in Palestine refer constantly to her boredom, worries, doubts, and alienation from her community. Yet constantly she remonstrates with herself, ashamed of her complaints and doubts:

> I'm ashamed of myself for complaining, but can't rid myself of the belief that precious years have been wasted, years that should be devoted to study and self-improvement. . . .
>
> That's a lie! cries another voice. I'm studying, learning about life.
>
> That's not true either. I live in a world of my own making, without any contact with the

outside world. I live here like a drop of oil on water, sometimes afloat, sometimes submerged, but always remaining apart. . . .

I can think of nothing now but my mother and brother. I am sometimes overwhelmed by dreadful fears. Will we ever meet again?

In January 1943, she confided to her diary that she had decided to return to Hungary to rescue her mother and bring her to Palestine. Not long after, she received a visit from a young man, a member of the Palmach, the commando unit of the Haganah, the underground Jewish defense force. He told her that the Haganah had for many months urged the British to recruit a force of Jewish paratroopers to help the resistance in Eastern Europe and to rescue Jews. The British had not been particularly interested in aiding the rescue of European Jewry and had rebuffed the suggestions. But after hundreds of Allied airmen had been shot down and captured over Romania, the British decided they needed better intelligence on German air defenses and had recently warmed to the idea of Jewish paratroopers helping them in that endeavor. If they would agree to serve as intelligence agents, cooperate with local resistance fighters, and help captured airmen escape before they turned their attention to rescuing Jews, the British would train, supply, and transport them to Eastern Europe.

Hannah begged the young man to recommend her to the Haganah. Two months later, he returned to let her know the British had approved the mission and that he had submitted her name for an interview in Tel Aviv. By the end of June, 240 volunteers, mostly men but a few women, were selected for training as paratroopers in the British army. Thirty-two of them would be sent to the Balkans, among them Hannah Senesh.

Three months of training followed, beginning in December 1943: first, basic training, where the volunteers were instructed in hand-to-hand combat and small-weapons use; then, parachute jumping; and, finally, to Cairo, for training in the arts of spying and sabotage. The day before Hannah departed for Cairo, she learned that her brother, whom she had not seen for six years and with whom she had lost all contact, had arrived in Haifa after enduring months in prison, escaping France, and crossing Spain. She raced to meet him and, using her credentials as a British officer, got him released from an internment camp. Although overjoyed to be reunited with her brother, she spent exactly one day with him. The next day, without telling him the reason for her departure, she left for Cairo.

Hannah concluded her diary as she prepared to leave Tel Aviv for Cairo, her last entry recorded on January 11, 1944:

I want to believe that what I've done, and will do, are right. Time will tell the rest.

While she and her associates prepared in Cairo for their mission to Hungary, the course of the war's events in her birthplace took a turn for the worse. The Hungarian government had begun to fear the advance of the Red Army and was becoming a less stalwart Nazi ally, even in the matter closest to the heart of the Third Reich, the internment and elimination of European Jewry. Anticipating the imminent German occupation of Hungary, the British informed the Jewish volunteers that their mission would be delayed for some weeks, and when they did deploy it would be to Yugoslavia, not Hungary. No one was more frustrated than Hannah, who meant to go to Hungary and rescue Jews, no matter what the British expected her to do.

Finally, on March 10 they were flown to Italy, and three days later they parachuted into Yugoslavia. "Mother Darling," she wrote in a letter that day, "In a few days I'll be so close—and yet so far. Forgive me, and try to understand."

But the few days turned into

three months. Hannah and her small unit made contact immediately with the Yugoslav resistance and spent many weeks in action with various partisan bands, traveling from village to village, fighting Germans and then disappearing into the forests. Always, Hannah pressed the partisans to help them reach and cross the Hungarian border. But their British superiors withheld permission, ordering them to remain in Yugoslavia and help the resistance there. The partisans had little interest in helping her. They had their own mission, their own dangers to face. Her comrades had more respect for their chain of command than Hannah, who believed she answered to a higher authority than the British army. And they were more cautious than Hannah. They wanted to rescue their fellow Jews, too, and they were brave. But they didn't think it wise to take unnecessary risks. The necessary ones were dangerous enough.

Two of her fellow commandos, Yoel Palgi and Reuven Dafne, who had trained with her and served alongside her in Yugoslavia remember her as argumentative, impatient, reckless, and vexing. Both in Cairo and in Yugoslavia they wondered how they would ever be able to work with her. "Our chief rebel," Palgi recalls. "And she was not always right."

They both loved her, worried for her, argued with her, became frustrated with her hectoring insistence that they do what they had come to do. But they respected her, too, and accepted her as their leader, her authority derived not from her commission as a radio officer in the British army, a rank that wasn't superior to theirs, but from the force of her personality.

Dafne and Hannah had jumped together into Yugoslavia. Palgi arrived some weeks later, rejoining her "somewhere in the forests of Yugoslavia." He found Hannah changed, just as impatient and even more headstrong and argumentative, but more focused, hardened, more commanding. "Her eyes no longer sparkled. She was cold, sharp, her reasoning razor edged; she no longer trusted strangers." She had become a capable, levelheaded soldier, cool under fire, composed when others were not, and always focused on her purpose. Time and again she dissuaded her comrades from killing captured German soldiers in revenge for Nazi atrocities. "That's not what we came here for," she admonished them.

She wasn't any easier to get along with, though. She dismissed her superiors' orders. She thought the partisans were misleading them. Her friends argued with her, but to no avail. And she was right: They were being misled, as eventually became apparent to all of them. Hannah decided that it was time, irrespective of her orders, to cross the border. "Better to die and free our conscience," she told Palgi, "than to return with the knowledge we didn't even try."

She persuaded the partisans to take them to a village near the border and walked several weeks to reach it. Yoel Palgi went by a separate route. They made plans to rendezvous in Budapest. Reuven Dafne accompanied her to the village, but he would cross later.

When they arrived in the village, they didn't meet the escort Hannah had expected would take them into Hungary. It became clear to Hannah that the partisans still didn't intend to help her. When the four other commandos accompanying her decided to wait, she approached two young Jewish boys from the Hungarian resistance who had just arrived in the village and a French prisoner of war they had helped escape and persuaded them to cross with her. Fifteen minutes later, in the evening darkness of June 9, they were on their way.

Reuven Dafne had tried one last time to dissuade her. She refused and discussed with him where they would meet in Budapest. Then they walked, hand in hand, from the village for a few minutes before Hannah turned in the direction of the border and waved good-bye. Before they parted, she handed him a poem she had written a few days before:

"Blessed Is the Match." "If I don't return, give this to our people," she told him.

They managed to get across the border and reach a small Hungarian village without being discovered by German soldiers who patrolled the area in force that night. Hannah and the Frenchman waited with her radio outside the village, while the two boys went in search of their contacts who could supply them with travel permits to Budapest. As they approached the village, Hungarian police stopped them and began to question them. One of the boys panicked, inexplicably raised his own revolver to his head, and shot himself. They found the earpiece to Hannah's radio in his pocket. Local farmers directed them to its owner.

They tortured her severely, demanding to know her radio code.

She wouldn't tell them, not when they trussed her up in ropes, not when they beat her, not when they threatened to kill her. As they were transferring her to Budapest, she attempted suicide by jumping out a train window, but they stopped her.

She arrived in Budapest and was taken to Hungarian military headquarters. Her mother was waiting for her there. The police had collected her mother that morning and interrogated her before bringing Hannah to her—eyes blackened, bruises and welts on her hand and neck, and missing a front tooth. Her mother rushed to her, and as they embraced, Hannah asked for her forgiveness.

The policeman in charge ordered her mother to convince Hannah to cooperate and left them alone. But Hannah only assured her she had not returned to Hungary for her mother's sake alone. She didn't tell her why she had returned to Hungary, just that it wasn't for the reasons she was accused of. She told her that her brother was safe in Palestine. Then they embraced again until the policemen burst in to separate them and ordered her mother to return home.

Later that day she was taken to a Gestapo-run prison, where her captors threatened to imprison, torture, and murder her mother if she didn't provide them with the information they demanded. Still she didn't flinch even when the SS retrieved her mother and locked her in a cell with other Jewish prisoners. They would remain in the prison together for three months.

Hannah, naturally, became the other inmates' inspiration and source of comfort. She made dolls for the children held there with their mothers, even for some of the prison matrons. She somehow managed to learn all the important political and war news, which she shared in whispered conversations and in more elaborate clandestine communications with the other prisoners. She communicated with her mother and eventually managed to spend some time in her company. Yoel Palgi, who had evaded capture for two weeks in Budapest while searching for Hannah, was eventually apprehended and imprisoned there as well. They could see each other from a distance and communicated by mirror and hand signals.

With the Red Army already in southern Hungary, the Hungarian government prepared for surrender and the inevitable recriminations that would follow. Hungarian authorities refused to allow the Germans to extradite any of the

Hungarian Jewish prisoners, although nearly five hundred thousand Jews from rural areas had already been deported to death camps in Poland. They stationed Hungarian troops around Budapest prisons to ensure no others were deported.

With the end very near, Hannah's mother and all the prisoners felt renewed hope that they would survive their captivity. But in September, the SS came for Polish inmates incarcerated with Hannah and sent them to Auschwitz. Hannah was briefly reunited with Yoel Palgi in a prison van, where she told him what had happened to her. She was taken to one prison and Yoel to another. He waved good-bye to Hannah for the last time when she turned before entering the prison gates.

On October 15, the Hungarian

government was deposed by German-backed Hungarian Nazis. Adolf Eichmann returned to Budapest, from where he had fled some weeks earlier, to begin the final solution to the Hungarian Jewish problem. Within days of his return, the bloodbath began. Fifty thousand Jews were ordered to begin marching to Germany. Thousands died from hunger and exhaustion or were executed on the way. Hannah and two of her "accomplices" were ordered to stand trial.

Her mother, who had been released from prison, managed to secure the services of a distinguished attorney and to visit Hannah in the days before the trial. The military tribunal that judged her met in the prison where Palgi was held and where Hannah would now be held for the rest of her captivity. The trial began on October 28. The three judges presiding, like all of Budapest, could hear the sound of Red Army guns in the distance.

The records of Hannah's trial were destroyed, but an eyewitness has provided an account of her testimony. She stood to face her accusers calmly but defiantly. "I was born in Budapest," she informed them. "Here I learned to love the beautiful, to honor my neighbor and respect the good. The Hungarians were a beaten and suffering people. Through my love for them I learned to understand the beaten and suffering . . . and an understanding for all the suffering people of the world and a desire to help the weak."

She spoke of her father, who had been an example of "working for the sake of goodness," who taught her "to have faith in the good." She told the tribunal that they were the traitors of Hungary, not she. And they had better take care not to "add to your crimes. Save my people in the short time it is in your power to do so."

After the brief trial concluded, the judges must have taken Hannah's warning to heart. They stalled for time, announcing that they could not reach an immediate verdict and would deliver one eight days hence. Hannah was rushed from the courtroom building back to her cell. She passed her mother and embraced her until they were dragged apart by guards.

Her mother tried in vain to see her as they awaited the verdict. On November 7, three days after the tribunal had postponed the verdict again, she was allowed to see the judge advocate who had led the prosecution at Hannah's trial. She found him hurriedly preparing to join the rest of the Nazi government in their escape from Budapest. After first evading her questions, the man informed her that Hannah had been found guilty of serious crimes and executed that morning.

Yoel Palgi had heard gunshots that morning from his cell but had not heard the marching of a firing squad, the bugle call, the reading of the sentence, or any of the rituals that accompanied an execution. He and his cell mates were told that someone had fired a gun by accident. They learned the truth later that day.

The judge advocate, a Captain Simon, apparently felt one last call to duty and decided either to force Hannah to plead for mercy or to execute her without sentence to sanction the act. A young prisoner who served as a prison orderly was cleaning a cell near Hannah's when Simon confronted Hannah with the news of his decision. He recalled their brief conversation sometime later to Yoel Palgi:

"Hannah Senesh, you have been sentenced to death. Do you wish to ask for clemency?"

"Sentenced to death? No, I wish to appeal. Bring me my lawyer."

"You cannot appeal. You may ask for clemency."

"I was tried before a lower tribunal. I know I have the right to appeal."

"There are no appeals. I repeat: Do you or do you not wish to ask for clemency?"

"Clemency—from you? Do you think I'm going to plead with hangmen and murderers? I shall never ask for mercy."

"In that case, prepare to die. You may write farewell letters. But hurry. We shall carry out the sentence one hour from now."

She did as she was told, writing letters of good-bye to her mother and her comrades in prison. Simon would never deliver them. She must have expected this final deception because she slipped a brief note to her mother along with a poem she had written in prison into the pocket of a dress hanging in her cell.

One hour later she was brought to a courtyard and tied to a wooden post that had been planted in a sandbox. When an officer offered her a blindfold, she declined with a shake of her head. She looked up at the sky. The three-man squad fired their rifles.

When her mother retrieved her possessions later that day, she found the farewell note and the poem hidden in her dress pocket.

ONE — TWO — THREE

One—two—three . . .
    eight feet long,
Two strides across, the rest is
    dark . . .
Life hangs over me like a ques-
    tion mark.

One—two—three . . .
    Maybe another week,
Or next month may still find
    me here,
But death, I feel, is very near.

I could have been
    Twenty-three next July;
I gambled on what mattered
    most,
The dice were cast. I lost.

Before her body was removed to
the national military cemetery in
Israel, Hannah's remains rested in

the Martyrs Section of Budapest's Jewish Cemetery. An appropriate resting place, surely. But we have come by literary and religious tradition to see a martyr's courage as the defensive kind, like that of the Christians who accepted the horrors of the Colosseum, the approach of the hungry lions, for their faith. Hannah had not needed courage only to suffer stoically. She took up arms for her cause. Her outraged conscience required her courage to go on the offense.

She had exposed herself to danger for the sake of others, endured torture rather than betray her mission and her ideals, and ultimately made the last and greatest sacrifice a human being can offer. But, and I am intrigued by the question, is it accurate to claim that she surrendered her life for her people? Or, like the early Christians, did she sacrifice herself for the sake of something encompassing but also surpassing human suffering?

It's not clear from her diary or the recollections of others that Hannah had any firm religious convictions or that she even believed in the existence of God. It seems she had a chance to survive had she responded affirmatively to Simon's invitation of clemency. Had she done so, neither her mission nor the people she had come to rescue would have been any the worse for it. She was not asked, at least not in advance of requesting clemency, to betray a confidence or inform on her comrades. Did she really need to accept martyrdom for her cause? Perhaps Simon would have asked her for something in return had she said yes. Perhaps he would have had her shot anyway. But did she believe that before she spurned his offer so defiantly? That's not clear.

So we are left with the distinct possibility that Hannah sacrificed her life for her dignity and sense of honor, which included a regard for others more compelling than her own life but that might not have involved them at the end.

We can understand and relate to—if only barely—the sacrifice of the soldier who throws his body on a grenade to spare the lives of his friends. We might not be capable of such a sacrifice ourselves, but we might entertain the fantasy that we are. But who among us fantasizes he is capable of dying for a principle alone that doesn't immediately concern the welfare of others, but involves only his sense of honor as it affects his self-esteem? In such an extreme situation, wouldn't any of us risk surrendering a little of our dignity in the not unreasonable hope that the injury could be repaired after we had survived our current predicament? We might feel disgraced somewhat, but couldn't we recover from that by continuing to live honorably? What kind of courage is it that rejects such reasoning? Who possesses it? Who could fear that much an injury to his sense of honor that it prevents him from asking for his life? It is as mystifying as Roy Benavidez's supreme heroism.

Both Roy and Hannah clearly had a sense of duty, which they obeyed without qualification or hesitation. But Roy's heroism was, in the terrible moment it seized, spontaneous. Hannah had spontaneous courage as well, obviously, and perhaps it was manifested spontaneously in her last willing sacrifice. But it seems clear that she had courage on reflection, too, which seemed to prepare her for her fate. Consider her last poem, the one her mother discovered in her dress pocket. She anticipated her death, and though the line "I could have been / Twenty-three next July," indicated a longing for life, the poem also suggested a composed resignation to her fate. "The dice were cast. I lost." So matter-of-fact. Such an undemonstrative, unblinking acceptance of misfortune. Not "woe is me, I lost." Just a spare acknowledgment of the fact.

Was it sublime fatalism that produced such tremendous courage? I have a hard time believing that. Such a vivacious, passionate girl, so full of life, seems to me the very archetype of a lover of life, exuberantly alive to the pleasures and discoveries of experience, to all the good things that come of living a good life. I think she wanted to live, but on the very exacting terms she had set for herself. She couldn't live without something intangible but apparently essential to her. I don't think it was a conceit, either. I don't think Hannah wanted to die for the sake of having her memory exalted in history or to prove herself equal to a romantic image she conceived for herself. Her heroism wasn't a fashion. She made a choice to be heroic, but to be heroic in order to be true. Her purpose wasn't to die. She died for her life's purpose.

She resigned herself to death. Not in a spontaneous burst of courage, either, but on reflection well before the moment arrived, when she gave her heart to the kindling flame. Did she feel a desperate regret in her last moments? Who can say? It would have been the most normal reaction to her predicament despite the fact she chose it. All we know is that she made the choice, and accepted the consequence, without uttering a sound when death approached. She looked up at the sky and accepted it. Maybe it *was* fatalism that allowed her to die so gracefully. But it did not produce the courage with which she lived her brief life.

Fatalism can be a technique to summon or hold our courage or, more accurately, to keep our nerve. But more often than not it's an affected fatalism, a way to talk ourselves into courage. Like someone chanting to relax into a meditative state, we whistle past the graveyard, hoping that our false bravado will compose us, mask the outward manifestation of our fear, fortify us with something to get us through the experience without looking like a coward. We aren't really resigned to some terrible fate. We are simply layering over our dread of certain consequences with a veneer of courage, hoping that acting as if we had courage might help us master fear's paralyzing effect. We act brave to become brave.

When I've experienced difficult times or been in situations that portend uncertain or intimidating consequences, I usually find a little false bravado, a little affected fatalism, helpful. Somewhere in the course of my life, I picked up an incantation of my own, a made-up quotation that I attribute to Mao Zedong (for reasons I have forgotten long ago). "Remember the words of Chairman Mao: It's always darkest just before it's totally black." I used to invoke this proverb in more perilous circumstances than I usually find myself in lately. These days I am reduced to sharing its wisdom with my staff when we are discussing an unappealing political choice or a losing legislative strategy.

Though the occasions when I use it are less than heroic, its uses are the same: to affect a studied nonchalance, to appear indifferent to fortune, while persisting in a chosen course of action. It might increase my resolve, but I don't really need much courage for the challenges most frequently encountered in a political career. Political courage in our consensual political system is seldom all that courageous. The threats are rarely greater than a lost argument, an adverse policy decision in a country that can survive it, or defeat at the polls. Sometimes politics can threaten our reputation and tempt our honor. But most often the threats we face with political courage are disappointments, not lasting injury. And they're usually not the frightening variety.

Even people who try to conjure up fatalism to endure a genuine encounter with fear are not really fatalistic. They aren't truly resigned to all that fate holds for them. It's a technique, of some value, to help quiet their anxiety. Only mystics or people supremely confident they will soon enjoy the rewards of heaven seem to me to be capable of true fatalism, and the courage it gives them will never be possessed by the less enlightened of us.

A CAPACITY FOR OUTRAGE and a corresponding sense of duty to respond will more readily summon courage than will a pretended indifference to misfortune. Standing for or against something will often require and rouse courage. As it is the virtue that defends other virtues, it is aroused through outrage at an assault on our moral convictions. We should be careful to distinguish between outrage and anger, a distinction I've often missed. Anger might stimulate an impetuous courage, but of all degrees of courage that is the least effective. By outrage I mean taking moral offense at something. One of its byproducts might be anger. It quite often is. But anger that responds to a provocation (that might or might not amount to a moral outrage) in a pretty limited number of ways— an act of violence, an intemperate remark, a rupture in a relationship, a breach of civility of some kind—is something less than outrage. Sure, there are characters who are capable of a discreet anger, a controlled fury. But how many people have you met who are really capable of being angry and undemonstrative at the same time? Not many? Neither have I.

Outrage, which our sense of duty summons us to redress, on the other hand, can find expression in a wider range of behavior. We can use expressions that anger uses, or we can purposefully go about redressing the offense in quiet, civil ways, our comportment no different from what it is in other endeavors. I'll have to admit, I'm not speaking from personal experience here. But I've observed people who seem to manage extraordinary self-control without diminishing their experience of outrage. My outrage appears in most respects very similar to my anger, but with that one critical difference. Anger and the courage it can spark are depleted rather quickly. We blow up, speak our piece, swing our fist until retribution is accomplished, and then we move on. We blow off some steam and then return to an unexcited reserve or whatever manner we exhibit when we're not angry. Outrage, if we have a sense of duty, endures until the wrong is righted, as can the courage needed to accomplish the task. It goads us to action insistently. Even if our demeanor remains placid, our heart quickens and makes constant demands on our courage.

How do you build a sense of outrage and corresponding duty? Practice, I suspect. Considering that most moral choices in our society do not often risk violence to our person or even lasting injury to our professional or social status, we can strive to abide by our moral code without the restraint of overpowering fear. It may not be easy, but it's not usually terrifying, either. The child who rebukes a friend for cruelty to another might soon find the consequences were really not so terrible after all. On the contrary, other peers, not to mention the victimized child, might recognize the virtuousness of the act and be attracted to it and to its author. It should make it easier to take the risk of exercising virtue the next time. Then again, perhaps the child suffers a period of alienation from his or her friend and others. Maybe that alienation becomes a lasting breach. Even then the internal satisfaction of being good will last longer than the disappointment caused by the change in social status. Again, the experience should make the next choice somewhat easier. That kind of moral, if not courage, then at least resolve, unlike the physical courage of the soldier, is replenished by frequent use, strengthened by it, like exercising a muscle. We condition ourselves to have courage and the sense of duty that animates it.

No one can be sure of his or her courage in every situation. We can seek to make choices that require nerve to experience, hope it familiarizes us with the experience of controlling fear and makes it easier to find courage when we really need it. We can try to manufacture courage, act as if we have it, in the hope the pretense will summon the real thing. We can direct our anger toward a quick burst of courage. We can love virtue and deplore transgressions against it. But our courage may fail us anyway. It is the virtue that resists easy or repeated acquisition even by the most stouthearted, those with the most experience with it, with the best conditioning to acquire it. They might be the least likely to lose their courage, but we all have our limits.

The unpredictability of courage seems to have a sort of natural logic to it. Why shouldn't the virtue that ensures all the others be the hardest to possess? Aren't the most desired things always the most elusive? Isn't their elusiveness an essential part of their attraction? The pursuit of life's greatest treasures seems always to require us to tap inner resources we aren't sure we have to exceed our previous performance limits.

Yet we can expand our limits if we possess an ample capacity for real outrage, corresponding precisely to the extent of our love of virtue, a powerful outrage, an animating outrage. We will put ourselves in the way of its object deliberately and try to have the courage to remain there until justice is done. Unlike anger or boldness, such courage won't be limited mostly to the impetuous or spontaneous act, but will be deliberate and reasoned and won't necessarily disturb our self-control. Its purpose isn't an immediate expression of our feeling or just to master a fear, reasonable or not; it is to right a wrong. It lasts longer because it must last longer. We will rise up and hope our courage stays with us. And in those occasions, the occasions of heroism, it is less likely to desert us.

I met the woman her supporters refer to simply as "the Lady" in 1997. I was not prepared for her. I had never encountered anyone of international political stature who possessed such exceptional reserves of strength, such an extraordinary will, and yet whose demeanor was so gentle and delicate that it contradicted the imposing image of decisive, determined political leadership I had been accustomed to in my experiences with political luminaries.

Aung San Suu Kyi received me in a reception room of the residence of the American chargé d'affaires in Burma. I entered the room after she had arrived for our scheduled meeting. I first saw her perched on the edge of a sofa, smiling at me, so slight and diminutive that were it not for her arresting beauty, she would hardly be noticed in a crowd.

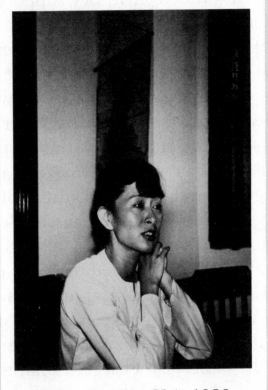

Aung San Suu Kyi, 1989

PHOTOGRAPH BY JOHN
EGGITT, © REUTERS
NEWMEDIA INC./CORBIS

Dressed in a Burmese sarong, a flower in her hair, composed perfectly in an upright posture, her hands folded in front of her, she presented an image I have never forgotten: a first and lasting impression of serenity and beauty. I was captivated instantly and remained so throughout our brief encounter. I'm a blunt man. My manners can be rough. Although I try to refrain from being intentionally discourteous, I am demonstrative in showing my displeasure. I am often impatient and can speak and act abruptly. I am used to dealing with people of similar habits and comportment. She spoke softly and paused before offering thoughtful responses to my questions. She was exquisitely polite and graceful, brushing my hand gently aside as I reached for a pot of tea on the table in front of us, pouring the tea for me. Could this be the woman who has caused all this trouble? I asked myself. Who has so confounded her enemies, the powerful, cruel men who unlawfully ran her country, imprisoned, tortured, and killed thousands, yet who seem completely befuddled by the implacable resistance offered by one gentle lady?

I had met some of those men on my first trip to Burma two years before, when I had not been allowed to meet with her. They were caricatures of third world despots, blustering, impervious to reason, dismissive of the civilized world's regard for human rights, and incapable of seeing themselves as the world saw them, as petty thugs and criminals whose brutality was inversely related to their intelligence. I had met with the head of military intelligence, General Khin Nyunt, one of the more public faces and leading powers behind the State Law and Order Restoration Council, the regime's chosen name, commonly referred to by an acronym that seems to have been borrowed from a James Bond movie: SLORC. My wife, Cindy, had accompanied me on the trip and to the meeting with Khin Nyunt.

SLORC had constituted itself in 1988 during a period of nationwide opposition to the military junta that had ruled Burma since 1962. The leader who staged that first coup d'état, Ne Win, had resigned during the largely peaceful demonstrations and appeared to yield power to a new government. Although many of the same figures remained in the new government, and Ne Win was still de facto head of the regime, the actions of the government during the demonstrations caused such an international uproar that the junta thought it wise to make some cosmetic changes. Various accounts accuse them of trying to quell the unrest by murdering between three thousand and ten thousand demonstrators. So they made a few personnel changes in the hope that things would quiet down. The new government was quickly displaced after a brief but bloody internal struggle by another group of generals. Ne Win's influence is believed to have been the power behind this new junta as well. They made a few other changes, renamed the country Myanmar, and, to everyone's surprise, promised free elections to choose a new national assembly as soon as order could be restored.

During our meeting, Khin Nyunt wanted Cindy and me to know that the regime had acted only to suppress violence and disorder he blamed on the protesters. To prove his point, he played a video-tape of a demonstration that appeared to have become a riot. There was no way to tell from the tape whether the violence evident at the event had been committed by democracy activists, as he alleged, or by the regime's own thugs. The latter was the most likely case, despite my host's protestations to the contrary. The civil unrest had been widespread but remarkably peaceful until the regime took extreme measures to put it down.

Our discussion had already lasted for more than two hours by the time he turned to the recorded portion of our meeting, long past the time when I thought anything useful might come of our exchange. I had excused myself once to use the bathroom and felt the need to do so again when he ordered the tape be played. So I watched, first with minor annoyance and distraction and then with disgust at the atrocities the tape had recorded. Among the confusing pictures of general mayhem—people chasing people, screaming, panic, beatings, and the like—were more awful acts of violence. One man was beheaded with a machete. When another was gutted with what looked like a long poker of some kind, Cindy ran from the room, and I demanded that the tape be turned off, to our host's seemingly genuine surprise. Our meeting ended shortly thereafter. I had learned all I needed to learn from and about the regime. I left Burma a short while later and refused the regime's invitation to visit again, unless I was allowed to meet with Aung San Suu Kyi.

Aung San Suu Kyi might disagree with me that outrage over the suffering inflicted on her people was the source of her extraordinary courage. Although she had lived many years in the West, she remains a devout Buddhist. She rises every day in the predawn for an hour of meditation. She protests that she does not hate the men who have turned Burma into an Orwellian nightmare and have imprisoned her for most of the last fifteen years. She will not hate them, she says, because she cannot fear what she doesn't hate. On the occasions when she has met with regime leaders to discuss her demands, she deferentially calls them "Uncle." Very Buddhist. I'm not sure whether the teachings of the Buddha warn against experiencing outrage as they do against anger and hate. Nevertheless, Suu Kyi clearly has a sound conscience that summons her to duty in the country of her birth. And I can't imagine how anyone with such a conscience and sense of duty could fail to experience a towering outrage over the crimes against humanity that her enemies have committed. Whether the outrage would arouse in anyone the courage that she has shown is another question.

Born near the end of World War II, she was the third child and only daughter of General Aung San and his wife, Khin Kyi. The "father of Burma's independence," Aung San had fought against the British, then with the British against the Japanese, and had worked with the British to establish the institutions of Burmese democracy. Several months before Burma's first parliamentary elections and the formal recognition of its independence in 1947, Aung San and several of his associates were assassinated by political rivals. Suu Kyi was two years old at the time. Her father's life and sacrifice is Burma's most revered national memory, a memory brought to life again in the minds of the Burmese by the serene dignity of his daughter.

Suu Kyi's mother, Khin Kyi, was a leading figure in Burma's democracy, serving her husband's legacy in a variety of government offices. She was appointed Burma's ambassador to India in 1960 and took her children with her to New Delhi. Suu Kyi attended high school there, where she studied the history of Gandhi's nonviolent independence movement. She moved to England in 1964 to attend Oxford.

While there she met a British scholar of Asian studies, Michael Aris. They were married in 1972. Their son, Alexander, was born a year later, when Michael received a post at Oxford as a professor of Tibetan and Himalayan studies. Their second son, Kim, was born in 1977, as Suu Kyi was settling into the life of an Oxford don's wife and writing a biography of her father. Theirs was the comfortable, interesting, rewarding, and well-traveled life of happily married intellectuals.

Suu Kyi had asked for only one assurance from Michael when they had married: "Should my people need me, you will help me do my duty by them." It was a promise both she and the good man she married honored in full.

Suu Kyi's family had made many trips to Burma to visit her mother during the first sixteen years of her marriage. She returned alone, however, in 1988, after receiving a call informing her that her mother had suffered a stroke. She arrived at the beginning of the Rangoon spring, as the nationwide protests demanding a restoration of democracy were getting under way. And it was during the Democracy summer that followed, when mass uprisings in August were violently suppressed by the regime and martial law was declared, that Suu Kyi heard the summons that both husband and wife had vowed to answer.

On August 15, the day bloodshed that claimed thousands of lives had ended, Suu Kyi sent an open letter to the regime demanding that they allow the formation of an independent committee to help prepare the country for the return of a popularly elected government. The next day, she stood before a crowd of five hundred thousand people, beneath a poster of her father, announced that she "could not, as my father's daughter, remain indifferent to what is going on," and assumed the leadership of what she declared the "second struggle for independence."

The Burmese people almost instantly took her to heart. She traveled throughout the country demanding an end to political violence and urging the establishment of a people's committee to help resolve the crisis. After the SLORC came to power and promised a free election, two hundred parties immediately registered to participate. The National League for Democracy (NLD) was formed, with Suu Kyi as its secretary-general. Because of her association with it, the NLD had by far the greatest public support. The SLORC, while promising an election, forbade political campaigns, outlawed public assemblies greater than four people, and continued to use force against demonstrators. Suu Kyi defied the ban and traveled throughout the country, drawing huge crowds of supporters. She repeated her demands for an end to the state's suppression of dissent, called for a campaign of nonviolent resistance, urged the United Nations to intervene to restrain the SLORC, and identified Ne Win as the power behind the junta. When her mother died in December, her funeral procession drew a crowd of thousands who listened to Suu Kyi as she pledged to follow the example of her mother and serve the people of Burma without fear.

The SLORC proclaimed her ineligible to stand for election herself and reiterated its prohibition on public campaigning, which she continued to ignore. In April, Suu Kyi and several NLD associates were marching with supporters when a squad of soldiers blocked their way. The soldiers were agitated and jumpy. They pointed their rifles at the campaigners, and the commanding officer seemed about to give the order to fire when Suu Kyi told her colleagues to step away from her. As they did, she walked past them, right toward the officer. Facing him, as placidly as if she were looking at a portrait, she held his gaze for a long minute. At the last moment, the officer ordered his soldiers to hold their fire, and she became Burma's national heroine.

In June, the regime placed her under house arrest for "endangering state security" and arrested many of her NLD associates, whom they tortured. Suu Kyi began a twelve-day hunger strike until she wrested a commitment from the regime that they would cease mistreating the NLD prisoners. Burmese law allowed the regime to hold her under house arrest for three years without trial, but in 1991 the junta extended it for five years and then extended it again. In the beginning, her family was allowed to visit her, but the government soon revoked that privilege as well, hoping to encourage her to leave Burma.

On May 27, 1990, the long-promised parliamentary elections were held and were, to the surprise of everyone, an accurate reflection of the public's will. For reasons unclear to any objective observer of Burma's political situation, SLORC leaders were confident of victory and stunned when they were confronted with undeniable evidence of the people's contempt for them. The NLD won 392 seats, or 82 percent of the vote. SLORC could claim a humiliating 10 seats.

True to form, SLORC simply dismissed the rebuke to its rule, ignored the election returns, refused to allow the new assembly to meet, arrested many of the election winners, and unleashed another wave of terror. At this point, Suu Kyi's likely fate seemed grim, and many feared she would join her colleagues in prison or worse. But her party's overwhelming electoral success, achieved in large part through her determined but strictly nonviolent civil disobedience, brought her international acclaim as Burma's Gandhi. The secretary-general of the United Nations demanded her release, as did many foreign governments. The regime reiterated its refusal to allow her family to visit and reinforced her confinement by denying her all outside contact. But her jailers were restrained from exercising more extreme measures to rid themselves of the problem she posed to their authority. That restraint became all the more frustrating when the members of the Nobel Committee awarded Suu Kyi the peace prize for 1991 and announced in their presentation statement that "we ordinary people feel that with her courage and her ideals, Aung San Suu Kyi brings out something of the best in us." The regime refused permission for her to travel to Stockholm to accept the award. Her sons accepted it on her behalf. But in an essay she managed to have published abroad at the time, "Freedom from Fear," Suu Kyi explained the philosophy that gave her the courage necessary to pursue her convictions with such unyielding resolve.

"It is not power that corrupts but fear. Fear of losing power corrupts those who wield it and fear of the scourge of power corrupts those who are subject to it."

Aung San Suu Kyi would not be afraid. She remained in her dilapidated villa, often without adequate provisions, losing weight, denied all contact with the outside world. But she confounded her oppressors with her calm refusal to be intimidated by their strictures and threats. She somehow managed to remain in regular contact with her political associates and even stiffened the spines of some NLD leaders with the rejection of their suggestion that events had forced the party to consider cooperating with the regime.

The UN Commission on Human Rights issued a report in 1994 condemning the regime for the torture and summary executions of its political opponents. That same year, Suu Kyi was allowed to meet with UN representatives, a few members of the U.S. Congress, and a *New York Times* reporter. She announced at the meeting that she was prepared to engage in dialogue with the SLORC without preconditions, which led to two meetings with Khin Nyunt. Little came from their discussions at first. But in the summer of 1995, the regime relaxed some of the restrictions on her. Although she was still forbidden to meet with other NLD officials or to travel outside the capital, she seized the opportunity to publicly reaffirm her demands for a peaceful transition to democracy. Large crowds of supporters routinely gathered outside her home to hear her offer dialogue and, at the same time, insist that political prisoners be freed and that the rights of political expression and organization be restored to the people of Burma.

SLORC steadfastly refused to allow another election, insisting that political rights could not be respected until a new constitution identified what those rights were. And the regime did all it could to make certain that the convention called to draft a new constitution would define those rights so narrowly that whatever practices it permitted would never achieve representative government. The convention floundered because of the regime's dilatory tactics and refusal to countenance real political reform, forcing the NLD to walk out in 1995. Suu Kyi pressed her case nevertheless, testing the regime's tolerance by attempting to travel outside Rangoon and by proclaiming to Burma and the world that her determination to wrest her people's freedom from the grip of unelected usurpers was as unyielding as ever.

In an inadequate attempt to placate world opinion, SLORC allowed Michael to spend Christmas with Suu Kyi in Rangoon. The welcome reunion of husband and wife would, sadly, be the last time they would see each other. A few months later, the government rearrested hundreds of her supporters and effectively abandoned all pretense that it was intent on securing a new Burmese constitution. Suu Kyi and other NLD leaders still at large responded by calling on the world to impose economic sanctions on Burma, a difficult decision considering the ever downward trajectory of the Burmese economy and the greater suffering it caused to a long-suffering people.

The call came at a most inopportune time for the regime, as it was negotiating with other Southeast Asians Burma's inclusion into the Association of Southeast Asian Nations (ASEAN) and the trade relations and regional legitimacy such membership would confer on the regime. So the generals cracked down yet again on the opposition, arresting hundreds more NLD officials, which in turn provoked new unrest as student-led demonstrations protesting this latest repression resumed and continued throughout the fall of 1996. More activists were imprisoned, and Suu Kyi once again found herself confined to her home and forbidden all public communication.

The world resisted her call for international sanctions, in some capitals out of concern for prospective commercial profits, in most, however, out of fear that the burden of aggravated economic destitution would simply be too great for the Burmese to bear. Even I, admirer though I was of Burma's nonviolent freedom fighters and their leader, worried that sanctions would punish the people more than they would convince their rulers to relinquish power. But the SLORC's bloody-minded depravity was just too despicable for respectable governments to refrain for long from accepting the necessity of adopting severe measures to oppose it. The United States imposed sanctions against Burma in April 1997. Europe still declined but eventually followed our lead after becoming exasperated with a regime that seemed utterly impervious to world opinion and incapable of adopting any trace of modernity.

The ASEAN countries, however, did invite Burma to join their ranks in 1997. And while SLORC's repression of political dissent persisted for the most part, Burma's neighbors succeeded in convincing the regime to make some concessions to international pressure. Suu Kyi was again formally released from house arrest, though still banned from political activities. The regime also abandoned its Orwellian title for the new, but equally ironic, State Peace and Development Council. Unimpressed with the regime's transparently absurd, Monty Python–esque attempts to spruce up its image, Suu Kyi ignored the restrictions imposed on her and resumed organizing political opposition. When she was stopped by police as she attempted to meet with NLD officials outside of Rangoon, she refused to return to the capital. They refused to allow her to proceed, and she responded by remaining in her car for six days until she was forcibly returned to her house. The next day she publicly announced her intention to leave the capital again and was immediately placed, yet again, under house arrest.

That same year, Suu Kyi learned her husband, Michael, had been diagnosed with terminal prostate cancer. The government refused Michael and their sons visas, and

Suu Kyi was told that if she cared to see her husband and make her good-byes, she would have to leave Burma. Had she done so, she could not have expected to return to the country she had been lawfully elected to lead. For all but a little of the previous ten years, Suu Kyi and Michael Aris had been kept apart by the cruelty of Burma's illegitimate rulers. Yet her sense of duty had been unrelenting, and she bore the separation and her loneliness with uncomplaining dignity. Now she faced a loss as painful as any physical injury could have been, almost as frightening, I assume, as one's own death. And were she and Michael to keep her promise to her people as faithfully as they had for the last ten years, she would have to forsake the consoling memory of kissing her husband a last farewell. Anguish like that surely affects a person as deeply as the most terrifying fear. Yet she had the courage to suffer it, a courage that for all its tragic consequences is as grand and noble as the courage of mythical kings. A powerful outrage must have assailed her fine, insistent conscience to have summoned it. As it must have summoned her husband, who bore his injury and grief with comparable dignity and resolve.

Michael Aris died many miles distant from his wife on March 27, 1999. Suu Kyi mourned alone in the house that was her prison.

In the years that have followed, she has kept up her courage. Burma's economy has continued to decline, and despite its oil reserves and other resources, the country is bankrupt. The United States and, to a lesser extent, its European allies have maintained sanctions on Burma's economy to register their solidarity with Suu Kyi and her people. The ASEAN countries have grown tired of the intransigence of Burma's autocrats, and even the more corrupt governments of the region have despaired over the surpassing corruption endemic in the Burmese government. In 2000, President Clinton awarded Suu Kyi the Presidential Medal of Freedom—the country's highest civilian decoration—in absentia.

These turns in fortune briefly affected the regime's resolve. After yet another return to the usual ritual— Suu Kyi is released; Suu Kyi immediately resumes her public crusade; Suu Kyi is rearrested—the junta, with the support of the aging autocrat Ne Win, again released her from house arrest and agreed to UN-brokered negotiations with Suu Kyi and her party. The regime subsequently released some, though not all, political prisoners, allowed the NLD to open offices throughout the country, and promised to prepare the country for a return to democracy.

And then, alarmed by her undiminished popularity, the generals changed their minds again. While Suu Kyi was campaigning in a remote northern province on May 30, 2003, her motorcade was attacked by a government-hired mob of club-wielding thugs who beat to death scores of her supporters. According to an eyewitness, Suu Kyi barely escaped the violence with her life. For nearly four months, the junta kept her locked in the notorious Insein Prison in Rangoon, allowing her only brief visits by a UN envoy and Red Cross delegation, who expressed deep concern for her health. Unyielding as ever, she began a hunger strike to protest her imprisonment and that of her comrades. She underwent gynecological surgery in September, following which she was returned to her own home, where she remains under house arrest as of this writing.

The generals, responding to international protests and sanctions, have issued yet another empty promise to begin preparing Burma for a return to democratic rule. Of course, their plan includes no role for the woman whom the Burmese have elected their leader, and to whom they remain as devoted as ever.

On her first public appearance following her release from house arrest in 2002, Aung San Suu Kyi apologized to her people. "I'm sorry to keep you waiting," she began. "But my freedom is not a major triumph for democracy; my freedom is not the object of our struggle."

So she fights on. And she will prevail. The regime must relent eventually. Suu Kyi and the people of Burma will rule themselves someday. The tyrants who have opposed and terrorized them for so long are simply no match for them. They lack their courage.

DANIEL WEBSTER SAID, "A sense of duty pursues us ever." There is nowhere to which we can escape our duty, our debts of honor. "If we say the darkness shall cover us, in the darkness as in the light our obligations are yet with us." The longer we live, the better we understand that truth. We all incur debts to others, and the obligations once accepted will trouble the most self-ish, hardened heart until they are fairly discharged. Our duty will chase us to the grave. So it is with the debts we owe to the brave, the obligation to repay courage with courage.

A cell mate, Bud Day, one of two men who nursed me in the first

In the Haktong-ni area of Korea, a grief-stricken American infantryman whose buddy has been killed in action is comforted by another soldier. In the background, a corpsman methodically fills out casualty tags, August 28, 1950.

PHOTOGRAPH BY SFC. AL CHANG, NATIONAL ARCHIVES AND RECORDS ADMINISTRATION, RECORDS OF THE OFFICE OF THE CHIEF SIGNAL OFFICER months of my captivity, who brought me back from the threshold of death, had that rare kind of courage, the kind that seems not only greater than his fear, but almost immune to it. He received the Medal of Honor for an escape attempt that was the stuff of legend, so heroic in the face of extreme hardship and peril that with all the bravado I could muster, with all the courage I hoped I would possess, I could never imagine myself being his equal. The prisoner who, after returning from an extended and brutal interrogation, didn't respond to my attempt at communication was one of the most inspirational leaders among us. He suffered more than many of us, resisted longer than anyone was expected to resist, and astonished even the cruelest of our captors with the strength of his courage. Lance Sijan evaded capture for six weeks after he was shot down. Shortly after he was captured—exhausted, starving, his leg broken in several places, his skull fractured—he attempted to escape. He was recaptured and tortured severely. No American was ever brought to Hanoi in worse physical shape. In terrible pain and delirious for most of his time there, he pushed on the walls of his cell, looking for a way to escape. When he refused to answer his interrogators' questions, he was beaten savagely for his silence. But he never gave them anything. He survived barely a month.

To this day, it is hard for me to remember these men, and many other men with whom it was my life's greatest privilege to serve, without experiencing a nagging anxiety that I am still in arrears on the debts I owe them. Their ex-

amples encouraged the rest of us
to resist as best we could, though
my best was considerably less than
theirs. They didn't demand our gratitude or admiration. They wanted
only for us to respond to their courage by living as bravely as we could.
They, more than my own resources,
more than any external assistance,
enabled me to return with honor,
the purpose we all shared and which
made our captivity easier to bear.
Debts like that are a privilege to incur. It is not just that I owe them for
suffering on my behalf. That's a serious debt, but not the greatest one.
The greatest debt I owe them is that
by their suffering they impelled me,
by inspiration, by the shame I felt
when I didn't measure up, to find
my own courage when I needed it
most.

Rare is the life that is not
touched, not obliged, by another's

courage. Surely we all acknowledge the debt we owe to those who risk their lives for our security, who stand a post between us and danger. But don't most of us, if not all of us, have memories of courageous people who are or were personally close to us, whose example informed our own understanding of the virtue, who introduced us to the values of honorable people and showed us the price that we might be expected to pay to uphold them: a parent, a friend, a teacher, a comrade? I think most of us know someone like that. It's been my good fortune to know quite a few, and the debts I incurred to them have been a happy burden to bear. I will never be as good, as strong, or as brave as they were, but I am a better man because of them, because they showed me how to live, because they showed me my duty.

No surer means to finding our courage will we ever know than to recall the courage that others possessed for us and the goading shame that chastises us when we prove ourselves unworthy of it. Shame hurts, but it is a useful wound, perhaps the most indispensable condition of a good life. Our self-respect, our salvation, depends upon our sense of it.

Thank goodness we have such debts, no matter how onerous they may seem, no matter how long they press us. We may never believe we have discharged them completely, and that may trouble our conscience to the end. But if we strive to make good on them, if we strive to be brave, there is adequate consolation in the effort alone, and those who love us will know we tried and be inspired in turn by our sense of honor.

So I'll leave you with one more tale of heroism, of a debt of honor incurred and repaid. It's the story of two men one whose courage was ready and extraordinary at the moment of its greatest test, the other, a frightened man who looked for his courage and found it when he needed it most.

Pete Salter commemorated every fifth of November by observing a vow of near total silence, and more often than not with a bottle of Scotch. From the age of twenty-three until his death forty-eight years later, it was the day he could not forget and would not discuss.

He was born and raised in the Midwest, the first of three children in a comfortably situated family; not rich, but not wanting for much, either. His father was a good man, firm but not severe, disciplined but not stiff, a hardworking, dutiful, and respected member of his community. He was the kind of man who expressed his love for his children through the conscientious discharge of his paternal responsibilities. But you could sense the warmth of his affection nonetheless. He worried over his children, was generous with them and just as quick to laugh with them as he was to discipline them. As his father had before him, he took care to instruct his children in the responsibilities of respectable people, offering them sound, unpretentious guidance that set down a wholesome code of conduct his children could see he kept himself.

His mother had been the more impatient parent. She could be selfish and sparing with affection, though her children loved her nonetheless. As Pete grew to be something of a handful, a little quarrelsome, and with a streak of independence that was not always wholesome, his mother thought instruction at a military academy might correct the small deficiencies in his character that had so taxed her patience. So off he went to Shattuck Military Academy in Faribault, Minnesota, for three years of secondary education. He learned something of martial discipline there, but his willfulness didn't seem to suffer much for it. He was a good-looking teenager, fairly athletic, and popular with both sexes. He smoked, drank, and broke a few other rules. He wasn't much of a delinquent, just a little given to misadventure, purely for the fun of it.

These were war years, and like most boys his age, he wanted to have a part in it. At the end of his junior year, he tried to join the Marine Corps. Since he was only seventeen, he needed his parents' permission to enlist. His father agreed, then quietly pulled a few strings to make sure that the navy and not the marines accepted his son into its ranks. Pete found himself serving as a seaman aboard a troop transport in the Pacific theater during the last year of World War II, duty less dangerous than the assignment he had wanted but that his father had worried might kill him. He mustered out eighteen months later, an electrician's mate third class.

He had finished high school and was nearing the end of his first year of college when an army recruiter offered him a chance to satisfy his ambitions for a more distinguished military career. With the promise that another war could not be too far off, and the prospect of an officer's commission, Pete Salter joined the army. Since he had reached his majority, he didn't need his parents' consent.

He left for basic training at the end of April 1950. Two months later, on June 25, 1950, the North Korean People's Army, the In Min Gun, crossed the thirty-eighth parallel, starting the Korean War. By September, Pete Salter was on his way to South Korea, the promise of a second lieutenant's commission forgotten. In deference to his previous service, the army made him a corporal with orders to join the Nineteenth Infantry Regiment, the famous "Rock of Chickamauga," then part of the Twenty-fourth Infantry Division, Eighth Army, Korea. His unit, E Company, had been one of the first sent to Korea and had already had a hard war by the time he joined it.

CORPORAL MITCHELL RED CLOUD was the best soldier in Easy Company. He, too, was a veteran of two wars and two services. He, too, had dropped out of high school to enlist in the marines. But his father had given his consent without thwarting his son's wishes surreptitiously, and Mitchell served with distinction as one of Evans Carlson's Raiders during their legendary "long patrol" on Guadalcanal. A qualified sharpshooter, he saw action in dozens of engagements before a bout of malaria sent him back to the States. After his convalescence, he shipped back out to the Pacific and fought on Okinawa, where a Japanese bullet earned him an honorable discharge, which he reluctantly accepted.

He returned to his home on the Winnebago (now Ho-Chunk) Indian Reservation in Jackson

County, Wisconsin, a warrior with a distinguished lineage. Both his parents claimed descent from famous chiefs. His mother's ancestor had been decorated for bravery by George Washington. His father had served in the army in World War I and came home to farm the depleted soil of Wisconsin lead-mining country. A self-educated man, he supplemented the family income by writing a regular column for some of the local newspapers. One of his publishers remarked that he "used the English of a Harvard professor." They were proud people, with much to be proud of.

They raised Mitchell, their oldest child, according to the traditions of his people. He learned to hunt with bow and arrow as well as a shotgun, and to fish, and while still a young boy he became proficient at both. He was taught the value of hard work, to respect his elders, to be honest, and to help others. And he learned from his father's example the obligation to answer his country's call in wartime.

He had been a quiet boy growing up, but after the excitement of war, life back home seemed too quiet and familiar. He was a warrior, descended from warriors, and the simple solitude he found hunting the woods near his home couldn't compensate for his sense of missed adventure. In 1948, his brother was killed in an accident while serving in the peacetime army. Mitchell decided to keep the family name on the army's roster. He enlisted and was soon on his way to Japan, where four of the army's ten divisions were stationed on occupation duty.

All four divisions were badly understrength and poorly equipped when Washington ordered Douglas MacArthur to come to the aid of the ROK forces, the outnumbered army of the Republic of Korea. He quickly assembled a small force of five hundred men, Task Force Smith, an insufficient force consisting of two rifle companies and an artillery battery, and ordered its commander to check the North Korean advance at Osan "with an arrogant show of force." They were overwhelmed and in full retreat one day after they got there. The next advance parties of the Twenty-fourth, including the Nineteenth Regiment, reached the port of Pusan on the southeast coast of the Korean peninsula on the Fourth of July. They were rushed west to reestablish and expand the defensive line that Task Force Smith had just vacated.

By the time Mitchell Red Cloud

and Easy Company arrived on July 12, the In Min Gun had pushed fifty miles south of Osan and the Americans had taken up defensive positions along the Kum River near the town of Taejŏn. They were quickly encircled by two North Korean divisions. They fought hard considering their lack of combat experience. Most of the division, like the rest of the Eighth Army, were raw recruits or draftees. World War II veterans like Red Cloud were in scarce supply among the enlisted. Few companies could boast more than a few. Most units were poorly trained and ill equipped, intended only for the relatively peaceful duty of occupying a vanquished foe. Though 95,000 troops strong, the ROK was even less ready for combat. The North Koreans, well supplied by the Soviet Union, had 135,000 men in the field: eight full divisions, two divisions at half strength, two separate regiments, and an armored brigade. They were tough, experienced fighters who had the advantage of surprise at the war's start and moved quickly, taking the South Korean capital of Seoul three days into the conflict.

Major General William Dean, the Twenty-fourth's commander, had organized the delaying action as best he could. It was a valiant but doomed effort. By July 20, Taejŏn was lost and the Twenty-fourth began to fall back.

E Company was in one of the toughest spots. The commanding officers at regimental headquarters judged it to be completely surrounded. Ed Svach, a twenty-year-old private first class in Easy's heavy weapons platoon, remembered it as the second-worst fight of his combat tour. "We were told to put our personal effects in a box that was to be buried, and were given the option of surrendering. But we didn't want to surrender. We'd already seen the bodies of guys who had been shot in the back of the head with their hands tied behind their backs. We figured we had better odds trying to fight our way through." So they kept fighting, taking heavy casualties, back toward Pusan. General Dean didn't make it. He was taken prisoner a few days after Taejŏn fell.

Lieutenant General Walton Walker, the Eighth Army's commander, hastily established a 140-mile defensive perimeter around Pusan, desperate to hold this last small piece of Korean real estate lest his army be driven into the sea. Easy took its place on the western end of the line along the Naktong River, tired, bloodied, and scared, but considerably more experienced than it had been a few weeks before.

Though it had suffered many casualties in its advance and faced numerically superior ROK and U.S. forces at Pusan, North Korea still managed to commit more men to the fight, conscripting thousands of South Koreans from territory captured in the first weeks of the war. It threw thirteen infantry and one armored division against the perimeter. However, with reinforcements arriving steadily, General Walker's men held the line for two months. Their defense was aided considerably by the use of American airpower. But Walker had also proved to be a master of improvised defense, while his North Korean counterparts were rather inept tacticians in comparison. They probed the perimeter in uncoordinated, relatively small assaults. And with an acute sense of timing, Walker shuffled his units here and there to plug gaps in the line, inflicting heavy casualties on the enemy and little by little draining the vitality out of the North's offensive.

In August, elements of two enemy divisions managed to cross the Naktong, creating a salient inside the perimeter, much of it in the Twenty-fourth Division sector. E Company and the rest of the Nineteenth were among the units charged with repelling the attack. The Battle of the Naktong Bulge, which continued into September, saw some of the fiercest fighting of the war to date. An entire North Korean division managed to cross the river before it was finally repelled. The Nineteenth took a lot of casualties, but not as many as it inflicted, and it received reinforcements, as green as they were fresh, throughout the last weeks of summer.

The North, its supply lines stretched many hundreds of miles and its forces diminished greatly, was being bled dry along the perimeter, while MacArthur sent another army division, a marine brigade, a regimental combat team, and four tank battalions into battle. ROK forces had regrouped, and Great Britain had committed the Twenty-seventh Commonwealth Infantry Brigade to the fight. The tide of the war was poised to turn, waiting for just one bold move to throw the North off the initiative and onto the defensive. MacArthur made that move on September 15, when he launched Operation Chromite. X Corps, consisting of the Seventh Infantry Division and the storied First Marine Division, stormed ashore at Inchŏn, the Yellow Sea port southwest of Seoul, and quickly overran its North Korean defenders. Racing east at great speed, it cut all the North's major supply lines before turning south. General Walker waited twenty-four hours for word of the landing to reach the North Korean forces besieging his perimeter before giving the order for the Eighth Army's advance north. After two months of a bloody stalemate, E Company was on the march again. Pete Salter had arrived in Korea in time to join them.

The In Min Gun was caught between two numerically superior, attacking armies. Within a week it was nearly finished as an effective fighting force in the South. Elements of the Eighth Army linked up with X Corps on September 26. Seoul was liberated the next day. Only twenty-five thousand North

Korean troops had escaped envelopment and managed to straggle back to their country. MacArthur initially ordered his armies to halt their advance at the thirty-eighth parallel. But despite vague warning signals from China not to enter North Korea, MacArthur and Washington could see total victory in sight. On the principle of hot pursuit and intent on unifying the Korean peninsula, President Truman authorized MacArthur to cross the parallel and continue his advance with two conditions: that no significant Chinese or Soviet presence be discovered in the North, and that only ROK troops advance to the far north where the Yalu River formed the border between Korea and China.

On October 1, ROK troops entered North Korea and raced deep into enemy territory. On October 9, the Nineteenth followed and ten days later helped to capture the North Korean capital, Pyŏngyang. Five days later they were north of the Chongchon River, fifty miles south of the Yalu.

China issued new warnings, but during the conference on Wake Island, MacArthur persuaded President Truman that Mao was bluffing. On October 24, MacArthur ordered his commanders to advance north as rapidly as possible. With any luck they would all be home for Christmas. The next day, as the first ROK troops reached the Yalu, and as X Corps withdrew from combat to prepare for new amphibious landings on the peninsula's east coast, an advance unit of the Eighth Army captured a Chinese prisoner. Over the next week, ROK and U.S. troops reported stiff resistance in the northern extremes of the Allied advance from what appeared to be

Chinese soldiers reinforcing the be-
leaguered North Koreans. Just
north of the Yalu, Mao had posi-
tioned a quarter million men whom
American reconnaissance flights had
failed to detect. Over the next ten
days, he would manage to slip
five divisions into the mountains
of North Korea. The Nineteenth
Regiment's E Company would be
among the first to fight them.

Pete Salter had just six weeks of
combat experience by the time Easy
had its first firefight with Chinese
soldiers. Until then it hadn't been
that bad an experience. The enemy
he had been sent to fight was in dis-
array shortly after he got there, and
the army's breakneck advance up
the peninsula had been pretty exciting. Easy had marched well north of
the Chongchon, not as far as the
Yalu but not that far from it, either.
All the talk was that the war would

be over by Christmas, and so far he had come through it without a scratch.

He had been in enough shooting fights his first weeks in Korea to feel proud of the combat infantry badge he wore and to impress the girls when he got back home. He hadn't panicked in battle. Killing North Koreans hadn't bothered him. It was a little hairy, but he had done his job as well as the next guy. They had lost more men on their way north, but not many. They were running a little short of ammunition, which worried him. C rations were running low, too, and he was constantly hungry. He had already grown to hate rice. "You would, too," he later remembered, "if you had had to mix it with coffee grounds to give it some flavor." Most of all, the "goddamn cold" was starting to get to him. An early winter was approaching, and though he came from the northern Midwest and was familiar with harsh winters, the cold in Korea seemed to bother him more. No doubt much of his discomfort was attributable to the fact that the troops were wearing summer uniforms. Their boots were unlined. Even their sleeping bags were made for summer.

Like all the men of his company, he looked up to Mitchell Red Cloud. An easygoing fellow, quick with a joke and always ready with a little timely advice for the younger guys, he was easy to like. The men called him "Chief," naturally. Although Salter was a veteran of World War II, too, he hadn't seen combat, not from the perspective of a decorated marine Ranger like Red Cloud, anyway. So, like the other guys, he watched Red Cloud, observed how he behaved under fire, and tried to follow his example. That's why Easy's commander, Captain Walter Conway, depended on Red Cloud so much. Not only was he the most reliable of his men in battle, but he could be counted on to show the other guys how to fight. Most nights, especially up north, he had Red Cloud on guard duty out on the perimeter. The guy had a sixth sense for enemy movement, and he could be counted on to give the alarm in time and to hold his position while the others got into theirs.

By November 4, Pete Salter and the rest of Easy had become good and tired of the war. For the last two nights they had run into Chinese, sizable numbers of them, and were getting beat up pretty badly. War is always chaotic even when it's going well. Now things had become seriously confused. They didn't know how many Chinese were hiding in the hills and mountains they patrolled. They never saw them during the day, after they'd gone to ground, pulling white tarps over themselves to melt into the snow cover.

MacArthur and General Walker still didn't believe China was in the fight to stay, mistaking their first offensive for either volunteers come to aid their exhausted fellow communists or just an elaborate bluff by Mao to spook them into backing off the border. Even after they had kicked the hell out of a regiment of the First Cavalry Division near the town of Unsan on November 1, Walker was not convinced that China had really committed to joining the war. The thing was nearly over. Why would they want to jump into the losing end of it? Nevertheless, Walker and MacArthur thought it wise to pull the Eighth Army back. Their supply lines were stretched pretty thin, and the forces north of the Chong-chon were becoming disorganized. Walker gave the order to fall back and regroup to prepare for a final offensive he and MacArthur were planning for Thanksgiving. The Nineteenth was ordered to remain north of the river to protect the bridgeheads.

That's where Easy was on the night of November 4, on patrol looking to link up with the other companies of the Nineteenth's second battalion. It had become very cold by now. They were all tired and on edge after the previous nights' encounters with their new enemies. They were trying to make contact with Fox Company before bedding down for the night, but something about the unusual quiet spooked Captain Conway, and he ordered the men to dig in on a little hill, Hill 123, five miles north of the river. Normally, Conway would have chosen a higher elevation on which to spend the night. The higher the hill, the easier it was to defend. But he didn't know how close the Chinese were that night or how many of them were out there. They could run into them any minute. The last couple of nights "they were in, on the flanks of, and behind the company position," he remembered. They couldn't even find Fox Company, though a full moon illuminated the darkness that night. He told the men to dig in quietly. "We don't want to draw any more mortar fire," he told them. "And stay on the lookout. They're here, somewhere."

As usual, he had Red Cloud with his Browning automatic rifle (BAR) guard the perimeter. He could trust him to stay alert. Ed Svach remembered how his friend claimed he always knew when an attack was imminent. "It's like hunting those Wisconsin deer," Red Cloud told him. "I can smell 'em coming." He knew his enemy. He knew they liked to swing around and attack from behind after a first noisy assault from the front. He was always ready for them. He didn't sleep. They wouldn't take him by surprise.

Pete Salter wouldn't sleep, either, and not just because he liked to keep an eye on Corporal Red Cloud for reassurance. It was too "goddamn cold to sleep," he remembered. Most of the men just scraped out a shallow depression from the frozen earth and then tried to get what rest they could. Salter decided to dig the biggest hole he could, all night long, if necessary, just to stay warm. They were all low

on ammunition. The company ser-
geants walked among the men, asking, "How much you got?" and the
answers were disappointing. "I got
two clips and a bandolier." "I got
three clips and a couple grenades."
"I got one bandolier, no clips."
They could already hear shooting
not far from their position, and they
knew it would be a long night.

E Company was near full
strength that night, around two
hundred men. But Ed Svach recalled that they were a bastardized
company by then, with fewer original members left than there were
replacements and men detailed from
other units to make up for the company's heavy losses. They were dug
in on the regiment's extreme left
flank. A five-mile gap separated
them from Great Britain's predomi-
nantly Canadian Twenty-seventh
Commonwealth Infantry Brigade,

also assigned to protect the Chong-chon bridgeheads. They were supposed to patrol the gap constantly to prevent the enemy from driving between them. But that was easier said than done. A mountain range covered the gap that made it pretty much a no-man's-land.

That's where most of them came from that night, swarming down from the mountains between the Canadians and the Nineteenth's second battalion. They drove in from the right, too, between the second and first battalion position. They hit all three forces that night in a coordinated attack all along the bridgehead line. Before they attacked the second battalion, they set up a roadblock behind it to cut off any retreat. Then they came up both sides of the hill around 3:00 A.M. on November 5, following the communications wire in the rear that led to the company command post. They completely enveloped both E and G Companies and caught most of the men asleep. They shot them where they lay.

Red Cloud was the first to see them and he shouted a warning from his position on the ridge just below the company command post. He opened up with his Browning and fired magazine after magazine into the enemy onslaught. The soldier feeding Red Cloud his ammunition was killed almost instantly. Red Cloud was hit, too, in the chest, but he kept on firing and gave Captain Conway a little time to try to organize some kind of defense. But it was already too late. They were overrun. Ed Svach, who had already had plenty of tough fights and would have others, remembered it simply as "the worst night of my life."

Pete Salter was still awake, still digging, when the night exploded with gunfire. As he scrambled out of his hole, tracers were firing everywhere; illumination rounds lit the sky. He could see Chinese soldiers shooting men near him in their sleeping bags. All was confusion and paralyzing terror. The men couldn't tell if they were firing their weapons at the enemy or one another. No one knew exactly what to do. On the very rare occasions later in his life when he talked about the battle, he did so with economy and with no bravado. On the contrary, he recalled his own actions with self-deprecating candor. "I wanted to bug out. I just couldn't figure out how."

He jumped back in his foxhole for a minute or two and began a brief but intense negotiation with his God, promising to live an exemplary life for the remainder of his days if He would just get him the hell off this hill. Few prayers were answered that night. But his were.

Red Cloud was wounded but still firing and staving off the complete destruction of his company. A dozen or more Chinese were lying dead or wounded in front of him when his platoon's medic reached his foxhole to dress his wounds. He didn't think Red Cloud's wounds were fatal and left him a few moments later to treat the other wounded. He came back after Red Cloud had been hit again, this time more seriously, and told him that they had to get off the hill or he would die there.

Ed Svach remembered what happened next. He was near the command post with another member of the company, Kenneth Bradshaw. He grabbed Bradshaw's arm and asked him who the hell was who out there. Bradshaw pointed to an opening down the hill and said, "Follow me, we're going down that draw."

Red Cloud had declined the medic's advice and managed to get to his feet, rest his Browning in the crotch of a tree, and resume firing. With another BAR man, PFC Joseph Balboni, he kept the enemy in a crossfire, opening up the draw so that those who were still alive and able could follow down the hill. Both men would die where they fought. And they knew it. Red Cloud would be awarded the Medal of Honor posthumously for his sacrifice; Balboni, the Distinguished Service Cross. The official account said Red Cloud had wrapped his arm around the tree to stay upright. Pete Salter remembered it differently. He and another man had managed to crawl down to Red Cloud, who asked them to help keep him upright. Salter got a web belt and wrapped it around Red Cloud and the tree. Then he shook his hand, thanked him, and started down the draw.

The fight had gone on for well over an hour by the time he began to make his way down, crawling some of the way, running when he could. He would hear the bark of Red Cloud's Browning all the way down.

Pete Salter had thrown away his rifle when it had jammed, and all he had for a weapon was his trench knife. Everyone who could was fighting hand to hand to get off the hill. He would, too, if he had to. He was fighting for survival, and most men will have the courage for that. It's the courage to deny that most powerful of instincts that distinguishes the real heroes, heroes like Mitchell Red Cloud and Joe Balboni. He was scared beyond any fear he had felt before or would ever feel again, begging God almost audibly to spare him. "Please get me out of here. Please." He didn't want to be a hero. He didn't want to be a soldier anymore. He just wanted to stay alive.

Before he got very far, he saw three Chinese soldiers approaching another Easy man's foxhole. He said he thought about it for a second. "I didn't have a rifle, and there wasn't much I could do." Then, for reasons he could never explain to himself, maybe it was Red Cloud's example teaching him once more how to be a soldier, he made his choice. He chose to be brave. The citation that accompanied the Silver Star he received for that decision reads as follows:

With utter disregard for his own safety he rushed at the leading enemy soldier and choked him to death with his bare hands. Taking up the dead man's weapon, he killed the second of the enemy soldiers while his comrade dispatched the third. He then continued to fight off the remainder of the advancing enemy as he withdrew to rejoin his unit. Corporal Salter's fearless actions reflect the greatest credit on himself and the United States Infantry.

He and the man he saved managed to get off the hill along with a very few others. Accounts of survivors vary, but both Salter and Svach believed only eighteen of Easy's original members got down alive. Red Cloud's gun had fallen silent a moment after they were down and Chinese soldiers flooded the draw, chasing after them. But by that time, nearly two hours after the attack had begun, four Quad 4s, armored vehicles with four mounted .50-caliber machine guns, had arrived at the base of the hill. They opened up on the Chinese, cutting down scores of them.

In the early morning of the next day, the commanding officer of the Quad 4s ordered them to help retake the hill. Initially they refused. "With what?" they yelled. "We haven't got any ammunition." But they knew they had to go back up. They could hear some of the wounded crying out. So up they went. Salter had barely started back when he was concussed by the explosion of a mortar round. Those who got to the top unhurt counted more than five hundred enemy dead, many of them lying a short distance from the body of Mitchell Red Cloud.

General Walker managed to get the rest of his troops back across the river, still not convinced that the Chinese were there to stay. And Mao briefly accommodated Walker's optimism. He ordered his forces back across the Yalu, ending what had been only the first Chinese offensive. Once his forces were regrouped, Walker ordered them to renew their advance on Thanksgiving, still planning to get them home by Christmas. The Chinese were waiting for them, armies of them. All American and ROK forces were knocked back across the Chongchon, past Pyŏngyang and past Seoul, finally halting near Osan. The marines of the First Division were trapped at the Chosin Reservoir in the northeast. Their heroic retreat to the sea is one of the most celebrated marine actions in their history.

Walker himself was killed in an automobile accident in Pyŏngyang, and General Matthew Ridgeway took command of the Eighth Army and fought his way back to the thirty-eighth parallel, where the fighting remained at a stalemate until a cease-fire was concluded three years later.

Pete Salter and Ed Svach had quite a few more tough battles to fight before their yearlong combat tour was over. But they never had another fight as bad as their night on Hill 123. They never forgot what was done to them there and what was done for them.

History records the official Chinese entry into the war on November 24, when Walker had renewed his offensive. Pete Salter grumbled about that a little. And he groused a little about how the marines, in their legendary retreat from the frozen Chosin, got all the credit for taking the brunt of the Chinese invasion. "The marines weren't the only ones there," he complained. But he never talked about any of it much after the war. Hardly ever, really. He would just slip off somewhere every November 5, alone with his memories. Every so often during the Vietnam War, a news report would trigger a memory, and he would make a cryptic remark to his family about how no one who wasn't there could understand what happens in a war.

He took his two sons with him on a business trip to Wisconsin in the mid-1960s. While they were there, he drove them to an Indian reservation to visit a grave, where he wept for a moment and then left without saying anything.

Mitchell Red Cloud's body was returned from Korea in 1955 and was buried in the Ho-Chunk cemetery. Ed Svach had escorted the body home, and he remembered his friend being laid to rest according to the customs of his people, with the sides of the coffin removed so his soul could escape, a bow and quiver of arrows next to him so that he could hunt in his heaven, and a bowl of fruit for the journey.

I doubt any man who survived Hill 123 forgot the man who had saved him. Pete Salter never did. Nor did he forget his promise when he had begged God to spare him and God had answered by anointing Mitchell Red Cloud his savior. He owed his life, and all that came of his life, including his children, to another man's courage. The debt might have seemed hard to bear at times, and he knew it would survive him and be carried by his descendants. But he knew it was a privilege nevertheless.

When he was dying, he told his son that God had spared him once, but he didn't think He was going to this time. He was worried that he hadn't lived up as well as he could have to his end of the bargain he had made nearly fifty years earlier. "I didn't get it right," he lamented. But he had. He had lived a good life in the years after the war, not a remarkable one, perhaps, but respectable, certainly respectable. He made a few mistakes here and there, but he worked hard, provided for his family, raised his children well, and loved them. And even had he lived a dissolute life, he should have known that he had kept much of his promise long ago, just moments after he made it, when in a terrible, terrifying moment, he made the decision to look for his courage and had not found it wanting.

WHAT IS INDISPENSABLE TO courage? Virtuousness, an active conscience, a love of dignity, a sense of duty that provokes the experience of shame when it is disobeyed, a perspective that ranks the objects of courage higher than its penalties, a capacity for outrage, a seeking nature, hope, the desire and willingness to have courage—these qualities and their exemplars I've admired and discussed—is any one of them essential to courage? Perhaps. Probably. They are qualities apparent in most courageous people. But I cannot say they are indispensable to courage without some reservation that I have overlooked other qualities, discounted other motivations that might produce it. If we can be certain of the origins of courage, could we not, then, be certain of our courage? Again, that is an assurance no one can have.

Courage is not always certain, and it is not always comprehensible. Roy Benavidez possessed many if not all of these qualities. He certainly had virtue and a sense of duty. But do they explain his courage? Would anyone equipped with an equal sense of duty show an equal amount of courage in the same circumstances? Cannot someone who loved his comrades as he did, felt a duty to come to their rescue as he did, experienced as powerful a need for courage as he did, have nevertheless assessed the odds of success as too daunting to warrant the attempt? Yes, of course. Few of us, even if we had his physical strength and martial skills, could have joined that battle, seen the hopelessness of it, and acted anyway. Once in the battle, the instinct for survival—a cause for which many, probably most, of us would find our courage—joined with his desire to rescue his friends and kept him fighting beyond the limits of human stamina. But wouldn't that same instinct for survival have kept him on the helicopter? There's just no explaining what made him jump. His courage was admirable, inspirational, but irrational. But, then, they don't usually give Medals of Honor for rational acts of courage.

There is only one thing that we can claim with complete confidence is indispensable to courage, that must always be present for courage to exist: fear. You must be afraid to have courage.

Fearlessness is a rare and inexplicable state of mind, a condition more rash and impulsive than considered. There are no lessons to teach it. There are no virtues that are certain to produce it. There is no training that will prepare you for it. Should you ever find yourself acting in a dangerous situation without experiencing any fear, an unlikely prospect, to say the least, you wouldn't be able to explain its origins any better than I can. Though I stand in awe of the few people who claim to have felt no fear as they performed a heroic act for which they suffered mightily, I'm not sure I can assign their heroism the virtue of courage. Perhaps they have some greater virtue than courage that is beyond my understanding. But as I'm careful not to define courage down, I don't want to define it up, either. Suffering is not, by itself, courage; fearing what we choose to suffer is.

General Sherman defined courage as "a perfect sensibility of the measure of danger and a mental willingness to endure it." That seems to me to be as apt a definition as any available. But I think we could use "perfect sensibility" to describe not only the awareness of danger, but the whole quality of courage. It is that rare moment of unity between conscience, fear, and action, when something deep within us strikes the flint of love, of honor, of duty, to make the spark the prayerful soldier sought. It is an acute awareness of danger, the sensation of fear it produces, and the will to act in spite of it. I think it is the highest quality of life attainable by human beings. It is the moment—however brief or singular—when we are complete, our best self, when we know with an almost metaphysical certainty that we are right. Having had it once, we would be greatly distressed not to have it again. I think God meant us to be courageous so that we could know better how to live, how to love what and as He commands us to love. Don't we all want to experience such fulfillment in our lives? And having experienced it once, who would ever want to live without it again? Isn't it worth the risk? The sacrifice?

On further reflection, maybe I can offer a less flip response to those whom the attacks of September 11 made so anxious that they no longer feel safe on airplanes or in tall buildings. Build your courage. This moment might precede a day when you will really need it. Get yourself ready for it. Revive your reverence for the values of a free society and the virtues of decent people. Have a care for your dignity. You're better than our enemies. You're not the kind of people who would murder to make a political or religious point. Our enemies sacrificed their dignity to their hate when they took innocent lives deliberately. We have something essential to happiness that they do not possess: a sense of honor. Keep it. However much you are afraid, keep it. It's worth your courage to defend.

We're part of a political culture that recognizes our dignity. That won't give us the strength of the merciless, whose actions are unrestrained by our values, by our identification with the whole human race, all of us born with an equal right to life, liberty, and the pursuit of happiness. But ours is the courage and the strength of the hopeful. Ours is the questing, optimistic spirit of progress, the search for answers to the great questions of human history: Why are we here, and where can we go? History shows that ours is the superior strength. We have something worth being brave for: liberty and justice. Feel yourself part of that grand enterprise, empowered by it, and dread the emptiness of a life that is unattached to noble purpose.

Pay your debts. The firefighters, police officers, and emergency workers who raced toward the danger that others fled, or tried to flee, bestowed by their sacrifice an obligation on the rest of us. The soldiers who embarked to distant, dangerous lands, to take the war to our enemies and away from us, away from our loved ones, bestowed an obligation on us. So, too, did the soldiers on Peleliu, in Korea, in Vietnam, and in all the savage battles in all the wars of our history. They are blood debts we owe. They're not a trifling thing. They should not be memories recalled just for our entertainment or to appropriate their glory for our own conceit, like the pride we take for ourselves from the hometown team that wins a championship. But don't think them a burden, either. Their recompense is our happiness.

Our fortunate birth, our blessed identity as Americans, this country, this culture of freedom and justice, the abundant opportunities here to improve our lives, to surmount class distinctions, to live in accord with the demands of our conscience, to believe ourselves as good as the next person in a country that trusts its success to the virtue and wisdom of each of us unless we prove ourselves unworthy of that trust—all these advantages preserved by the love, industry, and sacrifice of so many millions bestow an obligation on us. Our freedom will be secured by others, even for those of us for whom freedom means nothing more than the right to be left alone to waste our opportunities. But we have a moral obligation to deserve it. I cannot believe that freedom squandered carelessly is a means to happiness. Without that object, without the pursuit of happiness— not just pleasure, but abiding happiness born of the satisfaction that we have made the most of our opportunities, with all their attendant obligations and risks—what value is there in being free?

Not all of us will bear arms for our country. Few of us will ever rush into burning buildings to save others, or stand between criminals and their victims, or push beyond the limits of our current knowledge to conquer the misfortunes of our time. Not many will devote their lives completely to the well-being of others. Our country's success doesn't depend on universal heroism. Nor does our individual happiness depend upon proving ourselves heroic. But we do have to be worthy of the sacrifices made on our behalf. We have to value our freedom. We have to love it, not for the ease or material riches it provides, not just for the autonomy it guarantees us, but for the goodness it makes possible. And we have to love it so much that we will not let it be constrained by fear. It's love, then, that makes courage necessary. And it's love that makes courage possible for all of us to possess. We must love freedom for the right reasons. And, on occasion, our love will need courage to survive, to insist on our freedom. We'll need courage to be happy.

We have to face our fears and

make our choices in our circumstances to act or not, to love well or
not, to be brave or not. One in a
million of us, if that many, will need
to make the choice made by
Mitchell Red Cloud or Roy Benavidez or Hannah Senesh or Aung
San Suu Kyi or any legendary hero
whose mastery of fear seems to us so
far beyond our little spark of
courage to achieve that it transcends
human nature. They inspire us, not
to imitate but to admire courage, to
value it and to value its purpose. We
will face choices, not as dire as
theirs, but the quality of our lives,
the happiness of our lives, will depend on them nonetheless. And
what we choose will affect the happiness of others as well. It's misery
enough to live with the knowledge
that you are a coward. How greater
must be the misery to know that
you loved so little that the example

of your cowardice has weakened the hearts of your children, made their courage harder to find, their love poorer, their happiness more elusive? What other success could we achieve in our lives to overcome the guilt of such a failure? Nothing, absolutely nothing, could ever matter more.

All right, so you're afraid of flying and of tall buildings. It doesn't matter that you comprehend the improbability of the threat you fear. The fear is irrational, but no less real and affecting to you than were the threat truly imminent. Accept it. Accept the sensation of fear that our enemies have sought to provoke in you. Experience it. Imagine living like that all the time, how awful that would be. Dread it more than the thing you fear, and act. Put one foot in front of the other and move toward the thing that scares you.

You might tremble, perspire, feel your anxiety like a fever, the fear rising from your chest, constricting your throat, and swarming into your mind. I've felt it. Everyone has. But it's unlikely anyone will notice either your fearfulness or your resolve to act in spite of it. Our terror is never as manifest to others as it is to us. Just move along quickly and things will likely turn out fine.

If you do the things you think you cannot do, you'll feel your resistance, your hope, your dignity, and your courage grow stronger every time you prove it. You will someday face harder choices that very well might require more courage. You're getting ready for them. You're getting ready to have courage. And when those moments come, unbidden but certain, and you choose well, your courage will be recognized by those who matter most to you. When your children see you choose, without hesitating, without remark, to value virtue more than security, to love more than you fear, they will learn what courage looks like and what love it serves, and they will dread its absence.

We're all afraid of something. Some have more fears than others for reasons too various to quantify and examine. The one we must all guard against is the fear of ourselves. Don't let the sensation of fear convince you that you're too weak to have courage. Fear is the opportunity for courage, not proof of cowardice. No one is born a coward. We were meant to love. And we were meant to have the courage for it. So be brave. The rest is easy.

ACKNOWLEDGMENTS

Those readers who have found a few useful insights in this small book or inspiration in the brave lives it acclaims should know, as the authors surely do, that much of the credit belongs to people whose names are not boasted on the book jacket. First and foremost, we are indebted, once again, to Jonathan Karp, our wise and skillful editor. Jon conceived the idea for the book, and persuaded us that we were up to the task of executing it. His encouragement was indispensable to us, and his faith in us remains a cause of wonderment and pride.

Our debt to Flip Brophy, our

agent from the beginning of our adventure in the world of writing and publishing, and whose counsel and friendship we greatly prize, far surpasses our expressions of gratitude and her well-earned commissions for shrewdly looking after our interests.

We are also very grateful to Roxanne Coady for reviewing the manuscript and offering many intelligent suggestions on everything from the subjects we addressed and narrative pacing to trim size and price. Roxanne is the proprietor of one of the country's best independent bookstores, the much loved, hospitable, and successful R. J. Julia in Madison, Connecticut. The same virtues that have won her so many admirers in her community and beyond and earned her bookstore its sterling reputation—her superior business skills, wisdom, compassion, and deep love of books—are also the attributes of a remarkably perceptive book critic.

We wish to thank Mr. Edward Svach, a very brave man, for the sacrifices he made for our country, and for recalling for us not only many of the details of the battle on Hill 123, but for rendering with heartbreaking poignancy the terror and chaos of that bitterly cold November night over fifty years ago, and the extraordinary courage the men of Easy Company displayed in the worst fight of their war.

Thanks also to Commander Paul Gronemeyer, USN, for helping us track down the few maps and other records that still exist of the battles along the Chongchon River during the first week of November 1950. Marshall Wittmann gave us sound advice about style and substance, and, in particular, directed us to the extraordinary story of Hannah

Senesh, for which we are most grateful.

We are well aware how very fortunate we are to be published by Random House, an appreciation that grows stronger with our every experience working with the many fine people whose talent and dedication make it the premiere publishing house in the world. In particular, we wish to thank our publisher, Gina Centrello, for her strong support of the book; our former publisher, Ann Godoff, for her confidence in the project and in us; associate publishers Elizabeth McGuire and Anthony Ziccardi; our talented production editor Dennis Ambrose and copy editor Sona Vogel; editorial assistant Jonathan Jao, whose talents are many and especially impressive when tenaciously locating hard-to-find photographs; publicity directors Carol Schneider and Thomas Perry and publicist Jynne Martin, whose skills stand out even to those of us in a business famous (or infamous) for courting publicity; sales director Janet Cooke and her able team; and all the gifted professionals, too numerous to mention, who make those named above and us look as good as we can.

Finally, as always, we are indebted in so many ways to our wives, Cindy and Diane, and our children for their forbearance and support, and, most of all, their love.

ABOUT THE AUTHORS

JOHN MCCAIN is a United States senator from Arizona. He retired from the navy as a captain in 1981 and was first elected to Congress in 1982. He is currently serving his third term in the Senate. He and his wife, Cindy, live with their children in Phoenix, Arizona.

MARK SALTER has worked on Senator McCain's staff for fourteen years and is the coauthor of *Faith of My Fathers* and *Worth the Fighting For.* Hired as a legislative assistant in 1989, he has served as the senator's administrative assistant since 1993. He lives in Alexandria, Virginia, with his wife, Diane, and their two daughters.